Nigeria's Decades of Blood
1980–2002

—————————— VOLUME I ——————————
STUDIES IN CHRISTIAN-MUSLIM RELATIONS

SOME OTHER BOOKS WRITTEN OR EDITED BY DR. JAN H. BOER

The Prophet Moses for Today

Abraham Kuyper: You Can Do Greater Things than Christ
(trans / ed.)

Science Without Faith Is Dead
(Under same cover with above)

Wholistic Health Care (Co-editor: Dr. Dennis Ityavyar)

Vol. 1: Medical and Religious Dimensions

Vol. 2: Social and Political Dimensions

Wholistic Health Care Of, For and By the People

Caught in the Middle: Christians
in Transnational Corporations

The Church and the External Debt (edited)

Missions: Heralds of Capitalism or Christ?

Missionary Messengers of Liberation in a Colonial Context

For more details, see his Web site:
www.SocialTheology.com

NIGERIA'S

DECADES

OF BLOOD

JAN H. BOER

Essence
PUBLISHING

Belleville, Ontario, Canada

Nigeria's Decades of Blood 1980–2002

Copyright © 2003, Jan H. Boer

National Library of Canada Cataloguing in Publication

Boer, Jan Harm
      Nigeria's decades of blood, 1980-2002 / Jan H. Boer.

(Studies in Christian-Muslim relations ; #1)
Includes bibliographical references and index.
ISBN 1-55306-581-6.—ISBN 1-55306-583-2 (LSI ed.)

      1. Riots—Nigeria—History—20th century. 2. Nigeria—Religion—20th century. 3. Religion and politics—Nigeria—History—20th century. 4. Violence—Nigeria—History—20th century. 5. Violence—Religious aspects—History—20th century. 6. Islam—Relations—Christianity. 7. Christianity and other religions—Islam. 8. Nigeria—Politics and government—1960- I. Title. II. Series: Boer, Jan Harm. Studies in Christion-Muslim relations ; v. 1.

BL2470.N5B63 2003   261.2'7'09669   C2003-902372-9

For more information, please contact the author at:

E-mail: Boerjf@hotmail.com
Web site: www.SocialTheology.com

Essence Publishing is a Christian Book Publisher dedicated to further-ing the work of Christ through the written word. For more information, contact:
     20 Hanna Court, Belleville, Ontario, Canada K8P 5J2.
     Phone: 1-800-238-6376 • Fax: (613) 962-3055.
     E-mail: publishing@essencegroup.com
     Internet: www.essencegroup.com

DEDICATION

*This entire series is dedicated to two people
who have contributed profoundly to the perspectives
that have given shape to it.*

*The first and most special person is the late
Professor of Philosophy*

DR. H. EVAN RUNNER

*of Calvin College, Grand Rapids, Michigan, USA.
Professor Runner, I thank you! You have given me
what I and Nigeria both needed.*

*The second dedication is to the woman
whose support throughout this project has been
beyond description:*

FRANCES ANN PRINS-BOER

*Famke, you and your patience, help and support
are amazing! Thank you!*

TABLE OF CONTENTS

Appendices

ABBREVIATIONS

ABU	Ahmadu Bello University
CAN	Christian Association of Nigeria
CC	*Christian Courier*
COCIN	Church of Christ in Nigeria
CRK	Christian Religious Knowledge (a school subject)
ECWA	Evangelical Churches of West Africa
EYN	Ekklesiyar 'Yan'uwan Nijeriya (Church of the Brethren of Nigeria)
JETS	Jos Ecwa Theological Seminary
JNI	Jama'atul Nasril Islam (Muslim umbrella organization)
MM	*Missionary Monthly*
MSS	Muslim Student Society
N	Naira, the Nigerian currency
NIPSS	National Institute for Policy and Strategic Studies
NN	*New Nigerian*
NS	*Nigeria Standard*
TC	*Today's Challenge*

TD   *This Day*
TEKAN   Tarayyar Ekklesiyoyin Kiristi A Nijeriya
            (Fellowship of the Churches of Christ in Nigeria)
TSM   *The Sunday Magazine*

ONE

INTRODUCTION

▲ THE NIGERIAN CONDITION

For some reasons perhaps deeply rooted in patriotism (however misplaced), hope or faith in the black man's ability to rule himself, youthful exuberance and a great deal of ignorance, Macaulay, Zik, Imoudu, Awolowo, Sardauna, Enahoro, etc., went to town demanding that the British must go. Nigerians sang for joy. We should have wept in self-pity....

With these tragic words Dele Sobowale greeted fellow Nigerians on February 19, 1995, on the front page of *Sunday Vanguard.* Sobowale shares this sense of desperation with millions of compatriots who wonder whether there is any light at the end of the tunnel that is today's Nigeria.

Many other Nigerian and non-Nigerian spokesmen embrace such despair over Nigeria's current plight. The cover of *Newswatch,* March 13, 1995, screams it out: "Corruption Inc.: Anatomy of Corrupt Practices in Nigeria." Another magazine, *Tell,* tempts potential customers with its cover which howls "Now, Nigeria Is

Finished" and "Secret Accounts: How Aso Rock Looted the Nation."[1] Karl Maier, a foreign journalist well acquainted with Nigeria, gave this title to his book: *This House Has Fallen.* The cries are legitimate, but the judgements are too hasty.

When the nation's top-ranking leaders need to assure the population that Nigeria will not fall apart, as did former Vice-President Augustus Aikhomo,[2] then you know something is desperately amiss. However, Nigeria has shown remarkable tenacity throughout all of its crises. Its continued existence can legitimately be called a miracle that defies all known categories and theories.

The late prominent Christian politician Jolly Tanko Yusuf affirmed Nigeria's "struggles against corrupt government and the determination of Nigeria's fundamentalist Muslims to make our country an Islamic state."

He even spoke of "the madness that has overtaken our country." The country's "gargantuan problem," he affirmed, "is corruption in government."[3]

Two former military Heads of State, General O. Obasanjo (at the time of writing once again President, but now in civilian garb), and Major General M. Buhari, have identified corruption as the country's enemy number one.[4] A good three years later, Buhari is still voicing similar complaints about "clear lack of accountability in the conduct of public affairs." In 1998, we read reports that the economy is being destroyed by an "astounding degree of embezzlement and perennial failure…to turn policies into projects."[5] In 2002, well into the third year of his civilian presidency, Obasanjo is still struggling against this demon that is proving almost impossible to exorcise.

When my wife and I first arrived in April 1966, after the first coup, we had good reason to wonder whether we would last a week. Our stay stretched out to thirty years, but the possibility of a sudden emergency departure never left us. We went through a civil war, many coups and innumerable bloody riots. We experienced the shift from subsistence to an oil economy subsequently ruined by outrageous corruption, extreme devaluation and an external debt burden that the people had clearly rejected. It left them in dire straits as they first saw their living standard improving significantly, only to see it plummeting. For the north, it was from tea, coffee and coke back to *kunu*. In spite of all the uncertainties, anomalies and suffering, we returned in 2001 to a Nigeria that, after a five-year absence, still had more than a residue of hope for its future.

It was not all negative—at least, not from a missionary point of view. During those thirty years, we witnessed unprecedented church growth[6] in the north, so that the Christian community caught up with Islam in terms of adherents and, according to some, surpassed it. The state structure had been re-organized so that the mammoth power of the Muslim government of the former Northern Region was divided over many new and smaller states with a view to giving the indigenous peoples greater self-determination. We arrived in 1966 to find a weak, uncertain northern Christian community that had little influence in the political arena. The Federal Military Government dared to rob the church of many of its schools and hospitals without fear of serious political repercussions. After thirty years, we left a numerically and politically strong church[7] that could no longer be pushed around by either government or Islam.

Neither was it all positive. Christian spirituality is faced with two major problems. One is the demon of corruption, with which I began this introduction, and in which Christians and Muslims alike participate—one of the two major reasons for Nigeria's woes. Efforts within the church to stem it have so far failed miserably and even been resisted, for it has penetrated the church at every level, even national.[8] The other is the subject of this study.

▲ CHRISTIAN-MUSLIM RELATIONS ————————

That other major national and Christian problem is that of Christian-Muslim relations. If corruption has demonized the country, these relations have bedeviled it.

I have decided to tackle this problem because I believe I have something to contribute. I have both the experiential and academic qualifications for such a study, but more, I have a deep concern and love for Nigeria and its people. As a missionary, I am naturally concerned about the health and vitality of the Christian church specifically, and that of the nation as a whole as well as of its Muslim people. As a theologian, I have high regard for Islam and deep respect for its adherents. I am intensely concerned that the adherents of both these religions should not cooperate in their mutual demise in favour of either a mass return to African traditional religion by some or an embrace of secularism by others.

I believe I have a significant if not unique message for the adherents of both religions. Both religions need to make certain commitments towards each other if Nigeria is not to fall apart or both religions fall into disrepute. **The essence of my message to Christians is "wholism," while for Muslims it is "pluralism."** In the case of Christians, they have inherited a dualistic secular approach from missionaries that is not only despised and hated by Muslims, but goes against the deepest intent of the Bible as well. I want Muslims to sit in and listen to this discussion. I want them to understand that they have been misled into identifying Christianity with secularism. Christians need to repent of their flirtation with the language and concepts of secularism, in an environment shared with Muslims, and move away from it by developing a more comprehensive, biblical world view.

At the same time, Muslims need to update their sense of pluralism. It is true that in the past, they have been more tolerant of other religions than have Christians. However, they have not kept up with contemporary developments, at least, not in Nigeria. The situation that developed a *dhimmi* class of second-rate citizens has now been overtaken, never to return. Nigeria is now marked by a pluralistic situation that no longer allows the domination of one religion over all the people. Conversions from both traditional religions and Islam to Christianity have produced a Christian community that is at least numerically equal to that of Islam and may well have surpassed it.[9] Such a situation calls for new inter-religious relationships; the old ideas simply do not cut it anymore.

In addition to changes in the religious makeup of the country, contemporary concepts of human rights and religious liberty clash with and undermine traditional relationships. Though the nature of both Christianity and Islam is to test the spirit of new ideas, rather than embrace them simply because they are there, neither can afford to ignore major sociological and religious population shifts as if they have not happened. Islam in Nigeria is in danger of doing the latter, while Christians fall short of the former.

Both religions have to affect changes in attitude towards each other. They need to move from hostility to respect. They need to develop willingness to listen to each other and to practice empathy. A sense of fairness and equality is badly needed. Both need to commit themselves unequivocally to the indivisibility of Nigeria and to the cooperation needed to make it a viable country again. They need to cooperate on basis of the justice to which both aspire in order to cleanse the country of almost total corruption. At the moment, there is a great risk that Nigerians will grow tired of all this religious ruckus and either return to a sanitized form of traditional religion or to an African version of secularism. This same world view, embraced by Europeans when they grew tired of religious wars, now threatens to overcome them. Today, especially in the USA and Canada, Christians are fighting the very secularism Western Christians themselves produced through their infighting. They are fighting what some consider a "cultural war" against secularism, the fruit of their own intolerance, for their very survival. I submit that Christians and Muslims are both potentially better off with each other than with secularism. Secularism tends to suck the lifeblood out of spirituality and has too many restrictive blindfolds to be viable in the long run. "September 11" was at least partially an explosive "No!" to secularism.

▲ A KUYPERIAN PERSPECTIVE[10] ─────────────

Most of my previous books have been written for and published in Nigeria. My readers, mostly Nigerians, will have noticed a certain perspective common to all of my writings. It is the perspective of a wholistic way of thinking that I have initially learned from the late Prof. H. Evan Runner, formerly a philosophy professor at Calvin College in Grand Rapids, Michigan, USA. The perspective is often referred to as Neo-Calvinism or Kuyperianism. This is a school of thought and social action that originated in the Netherlands, but that is now increasingly sought after by Christians from every continent, including countries like Korea, Japan, Indonesia, Australia, South Africa, Hungary, United Kingdom, various Latin American countries, Canada and the USA.[11] In all of these countries, this perspective is seen by a growing group of scholars and social activists as offering a viable arsenal of tools in the Christian struggle to develop and survive. Joel Carpenter, for example, has outlined the way this school of thought is influencing Christian higher education throughout North America and producing leading scholars.[12]

It is this perspective that underlies this book. It is a perspective as wide as life itself and world affirming.

As Carpenter put it, Kuyper's solution to the problem of competing world views—and that *is* Nigeria's problem—in his native Netherlands was:

to embrace pluralism and to emphasize the value-laden, commitment-driven nature of knowledge. He reasoned that people quite naturally formed communities of the like-minded that shared a singular view of reality, a distinctive pattern for living and a socio-political agenda. A just society would recognize this social, intellectual and religious plural-ism and encourage the various communities to negotiate the common good. Likewise, Kuyper insisted, one's knowledge of the world was inevitably coloured and shaped by one's prior commitments—most fundamentally, religious commit-ments—concerning the nature of reality. Knowing was never value-free; science could not be completely objective. Scientific naturalism thus had no claim to a privileged posi-tion over against other world views.

Kuyper was not calling for the fragmentation of public life, however. Given God's common grace, he argued, there would be much overlap in human efforts to understand nature and humanity, and thus opportunities for conversa-tion, debate and negotiation, both in learning and politics. Yet the social-intellectual and religious differences that drove outlooks and agendas were real, and they should not be forced into unitary national establishments, whether religious, intel-lectual or political. Various communities of faith and values could play public roles, yet not feel compelled to choose between domination, accommodation or withdrawal. They would have the social and intellectual space to work out their particular convictions, but would retain the right to put their ideas into play on an equal basis.

In addition to Carpenter's summary, I here add eight further items of clarification of some basic points of the Kuyperian move-ment that developed over time. They are selected on basis of their relevance to the Nigerian situation as per my judgement.

First, Kuyper developed his perspective in response to nineteenth-century secular liberalism in the Netherlands that had become oppressive and intolerant. Kuyper countered it with a type of *thorough-going pluralism* that would allow full scope to all groupings in society to blossom on their own terms, even the secularism that he considered demonic. This was starkly different from secularism that denied others the freedom to define themselves and sought to force them to live by its definition. Specifically, secularism invariably seeks to force religion into a straitjacket of private spirituality and individualism that restricts its expression to a so-called sphere of religion, that is, church or mosque. It seeks to reduce the scope of religion to the sphere of the subjective, while it regards secular knowledge as objective, neutral and exclusively suitable for the public square. Secularism has proved incapable of understanding the basic nature of religion because of what Paul Marshall refers to as "secular myopia."[13] Kuyper's form of pluralism would allow for the unfettered development of all religions or world views—note the plural—on their own terms, not as defined by secularism, though including secularism.

Second, Kuyper posited the *primacy of the religious impulse in human life*. The human race is, first of all, a religious race, a race of believers. This is in contrast to Rationalism, which emphasizes the rational as the centrepiece of human life. According to Rationalism, everything is based on an alleged objective, neutral reason. Reason is the neutral platform on which all people can meet and converse with each other. It is not a matter of "religion within the bounds of reason," as Kant would have it, but, rather, of "reason within the bounds of religion," as Wolterstorff of Yale put it so aptly in the title of his book.[14]

Marxism, another strong contender for human loyalty, emphasizes the economic aspect as foundational and sees all culture evolving on basis of economic interests. Empirically, Marxism is probably closer to the facts than is Rationalism. There is a close affinity between the influence of economic and religious factors, a strong mutual influence on each other. One can argue that there is even a kind of confluence of Kuyper and Marx here, for when people give priority to their economic interests, that interest has in fact become the centre of their religion and life—a new idol. Their religious life imperceptibly changes to accommodate their economic status. I have seen it happen in my own denomination with devastating results.

Kuyperianism focuses on religion as the basis of all human life, with religion seen as the point of ultimate loyalty and value in the lives of individuals and communities. All the other aspects are shaped by the basic categories of the dominant religion, faith, beliefs or world view in a given society. Of course, religion and the other aspects mutually influence each other, but when all is said and done, the foundation of it all is the religious or, if you prefer, faith or world view.

Among other things, this means that there is *no neutral zone* in life like politics, economic or science,[15] where we can all meet as neutral, rational people. Though Nigerian Christians sometimes seek a solution to the Christian-Muslim controversy in that direction, it is a lost cause, for all these cultural areas rest on that often-hidden foundation of world view, faith or religion.

Kuyperian Christians share this insight with both postmodernists and Muslims. They have, apparently, come to it independent from each other, though undoubtedly especially Kuyper and postmodernism are co-heirs of Western philosophical developments. One can even argue that both of them are co-heirs with Islam of Greek philosophy. Unfortunately, many Christians have been misguided into a dualistic scheme that separates religion from these other areas. The fatal implications of this dualism will become clear as we proceed.

Third, religion is not only the basis of a life, but it is also *comprehensive or wholistic* in nature. Again, this is an insight that

Kuyperians share with Muslims. Both traditions emphasize that religion is a way of life, not merely a slice of life or a sector that belongs to the realm of church and mosque. Both Kuyperians and Muslims produce books and articles exploring the relationship between economics, politics, and other cultural aspects to their religion and regard the latter as basic to it all. Both reject secularism, because it compartmentalizes religion and restricts it to a small area of life, to the personal and private. It squeezes religion into a narrow mold that does not fit its genius. Again, unfortunately, Nigerian Christians have by and large inherited a secular definition of their religion—an inheritance that has deprived them of more relevant tools in their relationship with Muslims.

Fourth, bare facts are inaccessible to us. *We all see facts through the grid of our world view or faith,* never as they are in themselves. We always observe through the colour of our lens. This explains why people with different lenses often interpret the same events in opposite ways, as if they are looking at different realities.[16] During colonialism, ecumenical missionaries on the one hand and evangelical missionaries on the other interpreted colonialism in opposite ways, though all were confronted with the same facts.[17] In this series, too, it will become very plain that Christians and Muslims interpret the religious situation in Nigeria in opposite ways. Though the objective reality may be the same for all, their world views drive them into opposite interpretations of the "facts." It is an objective of this book to aid both parties to look through the other's lens; if not to come to full agreement, at least to reach some degree of mutual understanding.

Fifth, the human race is appointed as God's *vice-gerent* or, as Muslims tend to call it, God's *khalifat.* Humanity represents God in this world and is expected to develop it. Christians know this command as the "*cultural mandate.*" Most varieties of Christianity have unfortunately downplayed this biblical teaching and separated this cultural mandate from the great commission—a separation that has also encouraged the trivialization of their religion. It is no wonder that R. Paul Stevens bemoans this "tragic separation of the Great Commission from the Creation Mandate," precisely because it has caused so much havoc in the Christian community. In fact, though almost all Christians know about the commission, few are aware of the mandate. In Kuyperian thought, this mandate is as crucial as it is in Islam.[18]

Sixth, Kuyperianism, along with Islam, recognizes an *antithesis* between the Christian or Muslim religion and all other world views. There is a basic foundational difference between these religions and competing world views that drive them into different directions and are major reasons for the different national and regional cultures of this world. This is an antithesis between the Spirit of God and all other spirits. Both Kuyperianism and Islam are keenly aware of this antithesis. Both are also aware of the fact that this antithesis can run right through the heart of so-called true believers, for all experience this battle of the spirits in their own lives when, for example, serious inconsistencies occur between one's official religion and her *actual* world view. Where such dichotomies exist, a person's behaviour will invariably follow her world view and usually go contrary to her official religion.

However, Kuyperianism also recognizes *common grace*, a term referring to the Spirit of God working in and shaping truth even in philosophies and religions that reject Christianity. The basic antithesis between them remains active deep down in the foundation, but it is relativized due to the fact that the Spirit of God reveals important truths to all religions and cultures. Because of this common grace, Kuyperianism gratefully recognizes many aspects of truths in other world views or faiths and is thus ready to cooperate with them. That is also the reason I appreciate so much of Islam.

The current mood in Islam, certainly among fundamentalists, is to emphasize the antithesis at the expense of common grace considerations. The result is a strong rejection of any truth in other religions and a militant affirmation of "Islam alone." It has led to a high degree of intolerance. No doubt, this current rejection on the part of Islam is because they have woken up from their colonial and secular slumber and are angry that they have been subjected to such humiliation. In the current atmosphere of anger and reassertion, there is little room for anything but antithesis.

Seventh, evangelicals and charismatics are very much steeped in individualism and concentrate on individuals, while their liberal and ecumenical counterparts have tended to be more concerned with communities and structures. The Kuyperian tradition will have none of these one-sided perspectives *and gives all their due—individuals and communities, people and structures.* The tradition has created structures in various cultural sectors that were to be guided by basic Christian perspectives. Christian newspapers, universities and colleges, labour unions, housing co-operatives and political parties have all been part of the history. The reason for these was the insight that all of these organizations are expressions of different world views, faiths, sets of beliefs and values. When the underlying world view is secular, this does not render them neutral but makes them pursue their goals along secular lines that exclude many Christian principles. Today, Muslims—especially the fundamentalist variety—are deeply aware of the difference between Islam and secular world views as they undergird the various social structures. Hence, like Kuyperians, they are in the process of establishing all kinds of alternative Muslim structures and write extensively about the differences they expect these to make for them.

Eighth, a major motivation for much of the above was Kuyper's *concern for the poor.*[19] His was not merely an abstract philosophical or academic concern. The vision surely included such marks, but underneath it all lay his passion for the poor and the oppressed. This is one aspect that has largely gotten lost in the subsequent Kuyperian movement. As the constituency moved up the economic and political ladder, the passion for the poor largely gave way for more middle-class concerns. In North America most adherents of Kuyperianism are found in academic and ecclesiastical institutions, where the philosophical and theological aspects claim the major attention.

Though Kuyper formed, among other institutions, a Christian labour union in order to empower the poor, today labour unions—whether secular or Christian—have rough sledding among most North American Kuyperians. I personally took up the challenge of empowering nurses' aides and other hands-on caregivers to Michigan's elderly by attempting to organize them under the umbrella of the Christian Labour Association. This was met, however, with a solid front of stonewalling in the Christian Reformed Church, the major heir to Kuyperianism in North America. Concern for the poor is expressed in typical evangelical fashion: charity rather than structural, as per Kuyperian tradition. After all, the homes for the aged are owned by members of this constituency and organizing their employees is seen as a threat to their economic interest and structures.

Every ideology, even the best, is subject to tinkering and emasculation when the economic status of its adherents has changed upward. Not only is Carpenter's quote above useful as an intellectual summary of major Kuyperian concepts, it is also illustrative of a changed focus in that it avoids any reference to Kuyper's passion for the poor. Kuyper was definitely ahead of most Christian leaders in providing structures that were effective in overcoming poverty in the long run. His was not the individualistic ameliorative soup-kitchen approach; he dealt with the structures needed to overcome the problem itself. The Kuyperian concern for the poor and related concerns for justice are very relevant for the Nigerian situation, and are an important point of contact with Islam with a similar concern for structures of justice and peace.

I introduce Kuyperianism into the Nigerian discussion because it gives Christians an alternative to the secular perspective they have inherited from missionaries who were not always aware of the issues or their implications. It is a perspective that is increasingly recognized internationally as pregnant with positive potentials for a Christian approach to the world and other religions. This perspective is hereby offered to both Christians and Muslims as a more legitimate interpretation of the Christian gospel that simultaneously is one that should make it easier for Muslims to live and work with. It could become the basis for more fruitful relations between the two faiths. It would enable Christians to withdraw the red flag of secularism they are constantly waving before Islam and that evokes so much negative passion in the Muslim heart.[20] Its contours will become clearer as we move along, especially towards the end of this series of studies.[21]

▲ PARAMETERS AND SPIRIT OF DISCUSSION ———

As to parameters for this discussion, Nigeria-wise, I will be hovering mainly between the 1980s and the initial birth pangs of the new millennium, though the post-colonial era of the Ahmadu Bello days will also come into view. The 1980s in Nigeria were marked by horrendous religious riots that continued throughout the 90s and have already taken us into the new millennium. With the adoption of the shari'a in a number of northern states in Nigeria, new tensions and even riots have already flared up—a process to which at this moment no one can foresee an end.

Though this project has been in the making for some years, this Introduction is being written during the aftermath of September 11, 2001. We have entered a new and uncertain phase in the relationship between the Muslim and Western worlds. At this very time, Afghanistan is being bombed daily. This book will not deal with those new developments. One has to place his parameters somewhere. However, these most recent horrible developments do indicate that Nigeria is a true microcosm, in the sense that it demonstrates the fatality of secularism in Christian-Muslim relations.

In contrast to what obtains in Nigeria, I promise to be polite and respectful not only *vis à vis* Christians, but also with respect to Muslims. I have some basic disagreements with both groupings, but I pledge my very best to remain courteous to all. That may not be easy for me, since I am an aggressive person by nature. However, I recently read relevant sections of John Bolt's *A Free Church...*, where Bolt writes about the American cultural war and indicates the importance of civility in such situations. Nigeria is in a similar war, not between Christians and secularism, but Christians and Muslims and between Muslims and secularism.[22] Such wars get very ugly unless the combatants remember the basic rules of humanity. In Nigeria, not to speak of the post-September 11 world as a whole, it has become ugly, very ugly, at least partially because civility has been thrown to the wind and the combatants are no longer listening to each other. In this discussion, I regard myself not as a combatant but as a self-appointed consultant to both sides, respectful, critical, civil and courteous. May I be forgiven for occasional signs of impatience or for remarks that may hover on the line between the humorous and the sarcastic. After all, I cannot deny myself completely!

I am an expatriate missionary holding both Dutch and Canadian citizenship. Some would say that this status disqualifies me from contributing to a solution to Nigeria's religious crisis. Being both a Westerner and a missionary, I am a member of groups that have contributed to Nigeria's problems. I will not deny those contributions,[23] but Nigerians themselves have contributed more during the past decades. I have not heard that for this reason all Nigerians are disqualified and have nothing to offer! Neither does my expatriate status disqualify me any more than other expatriates invited to Nigeria to participate in conferences dealing with the religious question.[24] I believe that with thirty years of deep involvement in Nigerian life, both as a missionary and a scholar, I have some useful ideas to contribute towards the parameters within which we must find a solution to our religious problem.

Now, I am definitely a Christian, not a Muslim. However, I have decided that I must allow Muslims to speak for themselves in these pages just as well as Christians. All along the way, I quote extensively and even attach appendices in which we will hear the Muslim voice. This is not going to be a one-sided tirade against Muslims. I will try to understand the Muslim community with empathy and not unceasingly criticize them—except where they deserve it! Where they are right, I will give them the credit. Where Christians are wrong, I will say so as well. My affirmations and critiques will cut both ways.

I am aware that such an approach will not be appreciated by some of my fellow Christians. Some will consider it a sellout. But this is what the Lord has put in my heart and I can do no other. I also realize that many Muslims will not believe my intentions and may regard this work as yet another ploy to undermine them. A Western missionary writing empathetically about Islam? That can hardly be fathomed, even though I am by no means the first.[25] I am out to proclaim the gospel of Jesus Christ, and I judge that this task needs a certain degree of objectivity and empathy for both sides if that gospel is going to get a chance to contribute to harmony, healing and nation building—and if Nigeria is to survive.

Note carefully that I offer some ideas about parameters within which a solution must be found. I do not delude myself into thinking that I have the solution itself. As Falola writes, "No widely held theories for curtailing the devastation of violence and aggression has been formulated."[26] When experienced, wise and gentle Christian leaders like Ishaya Audu throw up their hands in despair and confess that in this particular situation all solutions elude them, then it would be presumptuous of me to pretend to have ready-made solutions. But it could turn out that I have discovered certain perspectives on the Christian faith with which Nigerians are not familiar, that could help break the current impasse by providing a new vista of a more wholistic version of Christianity. That, at least, is my hope and a major reason for this study.

So, I humbly offer at least certain parameters that belong mostly to the aspects of the spiritual and world view. These are, after all, among the basic building blocks of both religion and society. The continued existence of Nigeria as one nation under almost impossible conditions is a testimony to her people's tenacity and vibrancy. It also confirms my faith in miracles! With apologies to Karl Maier, this house has *not* fallen—and does not need to fall. It is not inevitable.

▲ FORMAT DETAILS

This book tells only a part of the story. Plans are to produce a companion CD with greater details. In addition to more stories, this disk will include newspaper articles, conference reports, communiqués and government submissions from Christian, Muslim and academic sources that will not only provide a wider landscape but can also serve as valuable research materials for related studies.

Though eventually this study may appear within one set of covers, for now it will be published in the form of individual monographs, each unit dealing with a separate aspect of the subject. The title of the entire series of monographs is *Studies in Christian-Muslim Relations*. Each monograph will have its own title as well.

This Volume One of the monograph series, in addition to this Introduction, presents a detailed coverage of the religious riots that have dotted the Nigerian landscape ever since the early 80s. I try to give descriptions that are representative of the "facts," as the two religions see them in their own ways. Volumes Two and Three will examine Muslim and Christian analyses of the riots respectively.

So, an analysis of an analysis! Subsequent volumes will discuss various issues that cause friction between Christians and Muslims. Major ones are shari'a, secularism, wholism and pluralism. If time allows, there will also be discussions of gender and fashion issues, public preaching and mission, conversion and human rights.

So, a full plate and a well-rounded menu. All the way through, both parties will be given ample opportunities to express themselves through numerous quotes, some so long they will be attached as an appendix. It is common in quotations to indicate omitted sections by ellipsis points (…). For reasons of readability and esthetics, I have in some cases omitted these when they were too numerous. I assure you, however, that no meaning will be lost or distorted.

Though these studies are based on extensive and academically responsible research, they do not always follow current trends of academia. My aim is not primarily academic or theoretical. However, I have borrowed one leaf from that realm—namely, the abundance of endnotes. Some of the information may be unbelievable to some readers. It may be helpful and reassuring to see the source. The promised companion CD should especially help such readers.

They are endnotes with a difference. No traditional jargon is used and the notes often contain no more than is necessary to identify the publication in the Bibliography. For full information about any publication, you have to turn to the Bibliography.

Another non-academic feature is that I freely use the pronouns "I" and "you" to encourage a less formal relationship between you, the reader, and myself. It lends a more personal tone to the book. And personal it is: straight from my heart to yours.

May Allah, the Creator, the Ruler, the Compassionate, the Just and Merciful, known in English as God, bless us on this journey. I am not so unrealistic as to expect an environment without religious friction between these two faiths in Nigeria. I do, however, believe that both religions have the wherewithal to replace their current dangerous standoff with a more cooperative mode that will take Nigeria away from the brink. Failure to work towards this with the greatest urgency could not only lead to the fulfillment of the Maier prophecy, but also seriously undermine the credibility of the world's two largest religions. Neither stands to gain from either of these prospects. And so we pray....

▲ NOTES ────────────────────────────────

[1] *Tell,* 6 Dec/93; 30 Jan/95. Aso Rock is the Nigerian equivalent to the White House, located in the capital, Abuja.

[2] *New Nigerian,* 28 Feb/2000, p. 1.

[3] J. T. Yusuf, 1995, pp. xvi, 1-2.

[4] *NN,* 3 Feb/95.

[5] A. Madugba, Report from Association of Nigerians Abroad, 2 May/98.

[6] For a recent (2001) update on this subject see K. Woodward, "The Changing Face of the Church."

[7] In view of the church's extreme anger with Islam and its widespread participation in corruption, I am not sure I can legitimately add the category of spiritual strength to this evaluation.

[8] J.T. Yusuf, 1995, p. 99.

[9] Unlike previous censuses, the latest census did not include questions about religion. It has been suggested that the reason for this exclusion is that the government either was afraid or did not want to have it publicly acknowledged that Christians may now well outnumber Muslims. Both religions are claiming majority status and the rights that come along with it.

[10] This section, though important for understanding these studies, assumes advanced education. You can skip it if you find it too difficult. Do not let it discourage you from reading the rest of this and subsequent volumes.

[11] The most recent major publications on this subject in English are by the following authors, all listed in the Bibliography. John Bolt (2001), Luis Lugo (2000), James E. McGoldrick (2000), Peter Heslam (1998), James Bratt (1998). And then there is the standard work by Abraham Kuyper, *Lectures on Calvinism* (1931) and his monograph, *The Problem of Poverty* (1991). Kuyper, the father of this movement, wrote voluminously, but most of it in his native, not widely understood, Dutch language.

[12] Joel Carpenter, "Neo-Calvinism and the Future of Religious Colleges." Insert in *Contact,* Newsletter of the International Association for the Promotion of Christian Higher Education, Mar. 2001, p. 2.

[13] Paul Marshall, *Their Blood Cries Out: The Worldwide Tragedy of Modern Christians Who Are Dying for Their Faith*. Dallas: Word Publishing, 1997, p. 10.

[14] Of course, it is not only Kuyperians that hold this view. See e.g. Patrick Glynn, who recently argued similarly for the priority of faith over reason on a postsecular basis. See Bibliography for both authors.

[15] Jan H. Boer, *Science Without Faith Is Dead*. Jos: Institute of Church & Society, 1991. Here I demonstrate the dependence of science on faith and world view.

[16] I realize that this insight is not unique to Kuyperian thought. It is shared with Postmodernism. However, the latter is a newcomer. Philosophers can probably show a common ancestry.

[17] Jan H. Boer, *Missionary Messengers of Liberation in a Colonial Context: A Case Study of the Sudan United Mission*. Amsterdam Series of Theology, Vol. I. Amsterdam: Rodopi Editions, 1979, pp. 49, 218; *Missions: Heralds of Capitalism or Christ?* Ibadan: Daystar Press, 1984, pp. 23, 56.

[18] For further explanation, see Boer, 1979, pp. 491-492; 1984, pp. 150-152, 159-160; *Caught in the Middle: Christians in Transnational Corporations*. Jos: Institute of Church & Society, 1992, p. 2, Chapter 15; For a more recent evangelical expression, see R. Paul Stevens, "The Marketplace: Mission Field or Mission?" *Crux: Quarterly Journal of Christian Thought and Opinion*. Vancouver: Regent College, Sep/2001, pp. 7-16.

[19] A prime example of this Kuyperian passion is his *Het sociale vraagstuk en de Christelijke religie* of 1891. See Bibliography for an English translation.

[20] A few of my publications utilizing the Kuyperian perspective are listed in the Bibliography. The reader is also encouraged to check my Web site: www.SocialTheology.com.

[21] For a comprehensive systematic presentation of Kuyperian perspectives focused on Africa, I refer you to the body of literature created by B.J. (Bennie) Van Der Walt, retired Professor of Philosophy at Potchefstroom, South Africa. He has published an endless list of books and articles, but the most comprehensive is his *The Liberating Message* of 1994.

[22] I realize that I have just described the struggle in unilateral Christian terms. Muslims would characterize it as a struggle between

Islam vs. Christians *cum* secularism, since for good reasons they tend to identify the two.

[23] I have indicated the problems created by missionaries and other Westerners in my books as listed on my Web site.

[24] Olupona, p. ix.

[25] The writings of T. W. Arnold and of Kenneth Cragg especially come to mind here.

[26] Toyin Falola, *Violence in Nigeria: The Crisis of Religious Politics* and *Secular Ideologies.* Rochester: University of Rochester Press, 1998, p. 8.

THE STANDOFF

▲ Introduction to the Riots ─────────────

In this and the next two volumes, we are going to take a hard and detailed look at the long series of religious riots and related activities that have punctuated Nigerian affairs from the late 1970s right into the new millennium. The emphasis in this volume will be on the events themselves, while interpretations will follow later.

A hard distinction between fact and interpretation is mythical, of course, for we see facts only through the lenses of our own world view and opinion. Christian and Muslim reports as to what actually happened vary considerably, because of the differences in their lenses. For this reason, I regret that my Christian information sources about the "facts" of the riots are much more abundant than my Muslim ones. My materials on the various riots are a clear demonstration of the biased nature of the "facts." Part of the report is based on Christian "facts" and the other on Muslim "facts." The result gives the impression of two different worlds. Nevertheless, I will try to emphasize the event aspect of these developments as objectively as possible, while realizing that interpretation, especially selection, is inevitably involved. I will turn the tables around in the following volumes, where I will emphasize interpretation.

The emphasis will be on *detailed* facts—sometimes, on gory facts. The reason for such emphasis is not to create sensationalism, but in order to show the depth of hatred and anger these facts display. They show the profundity of the problems Nigeria faces better than any polite gentleman's account could accomplish. Inconsistencies in my own church have taught me that a theology that ignores the situation on the ground becomes useless and farcical, no matter how beautiful in theory. The resultant theology gets reduced to a bad joke. To avoid the same danger of politically correct but useless theories about Christian-Muslim relations, I will be dealing first of all with the way in which they relate to each other in real life. Some theories of the relationships between religions look pretty thin when confronted with the intensity and ferociousness of the hard facts on the ground.

The 9/11 event has been a wake-up call to reality and may well be the harbinger to the death of political correctness. As Anthony Wilson-Smith, editor of the Canadian newsmagazine *Maclean's*, put it: "It's tempting to paper over disagreements with comforting cliches, such as the notion that we all worship the same God…. But it's a mistake to ignore differences." Referring to comments made by Michael Ignatieff, he reminds Westerners that "the separation of church and state is strictly a Western concept; in most Muslim countries, the rule of law and tenets of Islam are intertwined."[1] Our differences are not only about modes of worship, but also about social, economic and political concerns that cannot be wished away or swept under the carpet. In Islam, these are all religious concerns—as they are to me, a Christian in the Calvinist tradition.

This chapter then constitutes the basic platform of harsh facts upon which rest all the subsequent volumes. To understand the bitterness on both sides in the rest of this series, you must constantly remember this dark chapter. If it seems long and somewhat repetitious, that is in order to impress every reader with the almost unbelievable chaos and hatred—and with the great urgency to find a way of peace.

Nigerian census statistics are dubious and fluid, but they leave us in no doubt that the two huge religious blocks facing each other are roughly equal in number. This has produced a dynamic that is totally unique in Christian-Muslim relations. "No other country can boast of the dubious distinction of having two such huge and equal blocks of Christians and Muslims facing each other with such profound mistrust and anger."[2]

An additional factor that makes for even greater volatility is that, though both religions are on the increase in Nigeria, Christianity seems to be outstripping Islam. Islam never had a majority in the country. That distinction used to belong to the traditional religion. However, Islam certainly had far more adherents than did Christianity until a mass movement in the Middle Belt[3] began to overtake Islam. Though the religious question has been eliminated from the last census, I have the feeling that Christianity is now in the majority. However, in this book I will not play the numbers game. I stand for justice for both sides. Nevertheless, the fear of losing out to Christianity has made Islam even more nervous, for it stakes its claims on basis of an alleged continued majority. Increasing nervousness spells greater volatility.

These two blocks are at such dangerous loggerheads with each other the country has several times tottered on the brink of another civil war. This religious tension is often cited as the other destroyer of Nigeria.[4] The almost desperate situation the two factors, corruption and religion, have created has made for deep-seated disappointment.

Though I am not about to delve deeply into past well-known conflicts between Christians and Muslims, such as the Crusades and colonialism,[5] it should be realized that the resentment and suspicion these have evoked are still part of the Muslim psychological baggage everywhere, Nigeria included.

Similarly, the attitudes of Nigerian Christians to the events described in this chapter are seriously influenced by aspects of Nigerian history that are hardly known beyond her borders. First, there is the history of pre-colonial Muslim slave-raiding and hegemonies over their ancestors. Falola contends that the Middle Belt, the former theatre of those slave raids, was "a virtual slave farm."[6] Wiebe Boer, a Yale doctoral candidate in African History, informs me that at the turn of the twentieth century, the Caliphate of Sokoto was the greatest slaving society in the world. Karl and Lucy Kumm, founders of the Sudan United Mission, graphically described the practice in their writings after witnessing it with their own eyes.[7] Second, the colonial policy of imposing Muslim emirs and chiefs on non-Muslim ethnic groups that had previously been independent from each other[8] created an internal local kind of colonialism within the larger colonial setup that eventually became the "remote cause" for some of the riots described in this chapter.

One can hardly understand the mutual resentment and suspicion of Nigerian Christians and Muslims towards each other without an awareness of those histories. So-called "radical" Nigerian Muslims frequently appeal to those Christian offenses whenever the former plans an attack either on Christians or on the government. Nigerian Christians often interpret current Muslim attacks and policies as mere continuation of earlier forms of jihads, slavery and Muslim hegemonies.

In the aftermath of the very rancorous Constitutional Assembly debate on the shari'a in 1977, a long series of riots occurred that started in the early 1980s and is continuing right on into the new millennium, up to the time of writing in May, 2003. I describe a number of major ones, while the smaller skirmishes are ignored here. The list grows longer by the day. It has ignored the millennial divide. By the time this series is fully published, it will certainly be outdated in terms of the riot list. However, even prior to the period covered by this book, according to a government report, there had already been over thirty "violent incidents of riots" in the northern states.[9]

▲ Types of Riots and Organization

These riots have had a number of different motives and shapes. Originally they were initiated by Muslims—though that is decidedly a controversial statement—while Christians sometimes started later riots. At times they are intra-Muslim affairs, with one sect attacking another. Sometimes they are by Muslims aiming at the government and could be considered political in nature, though a more accurate description might be "politico-religious," for religious and political concerns are never far from each other in Islam. At other times they are directed against Christians. In some cases, as in Plateau State, the riots begin as anti-government demonstrations. The resulting atmosphere of violence remains in the air, and later the riots become Muslim versus Christian, sometimes without a clear picture as to who took the initiative.[10] Eventually, as people became accustomed to violence and aversion to it wore down, Christians also initiated riots with the cooperation of traditionalists, as in Zangon-Kataf. Many riots spill over onto wider areas. Often the initiators can be identified, but in the case of Kaduna 2000, it is difficult to determine who started the actual attack. Usually a combination of motives is at work that is difficult to ferret out—but that is a matter for the next two volumes.

In terms of organization, I first tried to describe the various riots according to their type. After a while, I found that the situations were too complicated to allow such systematic treatment. Hence, I have resorted primarily to a temporal sequence, though even that became clumsy. I ended up beginning with the Maitatsine riot series on its own. Due to its unique character, it is best described as Muslim vs. Muslim, though many Muslims deny their Muslim status. The original Maitatsine riot in Kano also happens to be the first of all major religious riots in the north. I then turn to the other riots and treat them somewhat in temporal sequence. Somewhat. Where riots reoccur in the same locality, whether city or state, I describe the entire sequence before moving on to the next site. Thus, apart from Maitatsine, I start where the first riot begins: in Kano, 1982, and go on to describe subsequent Kano riots in 1991 and 1995 as well. Then I go back a few years to Kaduna State, where Kafanchan set the tone in 1987, thus starting more than a decade of unrest and bloodletting in Zangon Kataf, Kaduna City and, indeed, throughout the state. From here I back up once again and skip over to Katsina, 1991, and then on to Tafawa Balewa in Bauchi state, with its decade of outbursts from 1991 to 2002 and still going strong. 1994 is the year both Potiskum and Jos got into the act, with Jos and the entire state growing increasingly violent right on into the new millennium. Maiduguri comes in last with a riot in 1998. It was comparatively mild, but the issue on which it centred was a national one. So, there you have the menu for this chapter. The sequence is not without its problems, but it is the best I could come up with after several other attempts that turned out to create greater problems. This chapter deals with fifteen major riots.

▲ THE RIOTS

1. MAITATSINE SERIES[11]

Intra-Muslim riots are not the primary focus in this book, since they do not deal directly with Christian-Muslim relations. However, at a more remote but deeper level, there is an intimate relationship to that concern via secularism. In addition, the Maitatsine riots demonstrate all too clearly how ferocious the slaughter can become and how fierce. Hence, I merely summarize them. Later on, some Muslim apologists will refer to these events as the natural result of the secular regime introduced by colonialism and missions.

The December 1980 riot in Kano is a good—or, rather, evil—example. A sect called the Maitatsine unleashed a three-day riot in which almost 4200 people were killed, mostly Muslims. The purpose apparently was to reform Muslim worship and to cleanse Islam from its many non-Muslim accretions. Some Christians were also killed and many church buildings were attacked.[12]

Another intra-Muslim Maitatsine riot took place during October 1982, when the sect killed some 400 people in Maiduguri and destroyed much property. In the same month, uprisings also took place in Rigassa, Kaduna State and, again, in Kano. The government then banned the sect. But in February 1984, they struck in Jimeta, Yola, where 763 were killed and almost 6000 were displaced. In 1985, the same sect killed over 100 people in ten hours of fighting in Gombe.[13]

Of course, because of his claim to be a prophet, many Muslims assert that Maitatsine was no Muslim. That is a heretical claim in Islam. Abubukar Gumi, JNI and many other Muslims denounced him. However, it is correctly argued in the National Institute for Policy and Strategic Studies (NIPSS) report that "it cannot be denied that they have their roots in Islam. At the worst, they are probably a new religion spawned by Islam,"[14] not unlike the relationship of Jehovah's Witnesses to Christianity.

2. KANO SERIES

A. Kano, 1982

In October 1982, the Muslim Students' Society (MSS)[15] protested against the location of St. George's Anglican church in Fagge, Kano city, on the grounds that it was too close to a mosque—a situation that always offends Muslims. To fully appreciate the irrationality of this protest, you must know that that church had been there since around 1930, while the mosque was built between 1968 and 1970, some forty years later! The offense felt by Muslims increased when the Anglican Archbishop of Canterbury visited the place earlier in the year to lay the foundation stone for a new church building on the same site. The police successfully protected that church, but many others were destroyed and forty-four people were killed.[16]

Justice Haruna Dandaura, at the time President of the Christian Council of Nigeria and a native of Kano who was there when the church was built, was invited by the Kano State-appointed Committee to Investigate the Religious Disturbance to write a brief on the riot and its causes. In his submission, he summarized the history of the church in that area. In the irenic style typical of this man, he wrote:

> *In 1933, when the mission compound was built up, I was there. The compound then stood within the radius of about 1000 yards on each side from Sabongari and Fagge. There was no building of any kind anywhere near it.*
>
> *A few years ago the Waje Offices were moved…to somewhere near the mission compound. With this building came school buildings…to the east and north sides of the church.*
>
> *Right in front of the church, almost covering the passage, a court and police station are built. This appeared to have choked up the compound and there was hardly any way out.*
>
> *On the day the mosque was to be opened, Muslim worshipers filled the mission compound and worshiped undisturbed.*

Dandaura goes on to relate how the Muslim community benefited from these church facilities in many ways through the years. He referred to the "total condemnation" of the incident by the governor and the emir, but did indicate that such consolations are meaningless unless "the perpetrators of the incident are dug out and adequately punished."[17]

The Kano State Branch of the Christian Association of Nigeria (CAN) published a memorandum about this riot that also contains the substance of the memorandum they sent to the same committee to which Dandaura wrote his letter. The purpose of this publication was to bring before the public "facts which could otherwise have been swept under the carpet." Most of this memorandum is interpretation and will thus feature in Volume 3. However, it does list the nine churches that were destroyed during the ruckus as well as a Christian bookshop and "other Christian properties."[18]

B. Kano, 1991

Kano has been particularly vulnerable to riots. The October 29, 1991 issue of *Tell* screams out once again, "Bloodbath in Kano: Religious Fanatics Strike Again." Christians had invited evangelist Reinhard Bonnke from Germany for an evangelistic campaign scheduled for October, 1991, and had dubbed it a "crusade," a word that immediately rankles Muslim ears and reminds them of the crusades of past centuries. Previously, two foreign Muslim evangelists had been denied entry visas and a third had been deported. In addition, Muslims were denied the use of the Race Course for one of their celebrations, while Bonnke's crusade was originally scheduled to be held there. The riot that ensued killed hundreds of people. Over sixty Christian businesses and allegedly more than twenty churches were destroyed. In order to give you a flavour of the atmosphere in the city, I treat you to selected passages from Dare Babarinsa's account of the flow of events after the arrival of Bonnke.[19]

> *Around 10 a.m., about 8,000 Muslim youths marched to the emir's palace. They were protesting the presence of Bonnke, whom they accused of planning to blaspheme Islam. The protesters, who were led by Islamic clerics, demanded to see the emir. The Wamba Kano promised that the crusade "will not*

be allowed to take place in Kano." After noon prayer, the peaceful protest became a mob action. It took on a life of its own, descending on the city like a bestial thunderstorm. By this time, the demonstration had been taken over by fundamentalists. Amidst the battle cry of Allah Akbar!, for Kano and Nigerians, a familiar nightmare was repeating itself.

The riot lasted two days, leaving more than 200 people dead and hundreds injured. The governor imposed a 12-hour curfew on the city…. President Babangida, who was attending the Commonwealth summit in…Zimbabwe, hurried home to take charge of the situation.

The targets were mostly southerners and Christian northerners. As the rioters moved from street to street, killing people, setting vehicles and houses on fire, a new dimension was introduced. As had never happened in previous riots, the Christian community showed an unwillingness to turn the other cheek. They mounted barricades and formed vigilante groups to defend the non-indigene enclave of Sabon Gari. Rings of fire, from burning tires and other materials, were placed on many roads in Sabon Gari….

But before the defenders got their act together, the destruction had been massive and far-reaching. …Building materials worth millions of naira were destroyed and looted. Corpses littered the areas. As Sabon Gari became a well-defended fortress, the fundamentalists moved to pockets of non-indigenous settlements and houses in other parts of the…city and rounded the people up.

The counter-attack threatened to escalate the crisis. A mosque was burnt at Emir Road in apparent retaliation for the more than 20 churches burnt. The terrible destruction was more visible on Airport Road where a big Mobil filling station was burnt and 16 vehicles were burnt at a nearby Total filling station. Another Agip station was burnt. The famous Queen's

> *Cinema as well as the headquarters of Kabo Holdings, which*
> *houses a branch of the Bank of the North, were also gutted.*

What baffled security men and government officials was the
ferocity of the uprising. It was clear the security agencies were
aware that there might be trouble. Many weeks before, the state
government received an application from CAN asking for the use
of the Race Course for the use of Bonnke's one-week crusade. CAN
was asked to pay the mandatory fee of N10,000. But as security
reports reached the government, it found itself on the horns of a
dilemma. Bonnke was not a newcomer to Nigeria. During his previous crusades in several Nigerian cities, the charismatic preacher
was able to convert many to Christianity. Now he was coming to
Kano to perform his expected feat. At this point, Babarinsa gives a
summary of previous riots and their effects on Kano, all clear evi-
dences of the volatility of the place. He then goes on as follows:

> *All these antecedents made the security agencies uneasy*
> *about Bonnke. It was decided that, in order not to antago-*
> *nize the Christians, the visit should be managed in a low*
> *profile manner. In order to persuade CAN to hold the rally*
> *in a less conspicuous place, the government suddenly*
> *increased the fee to N30,000 and later N50,000. When*
> *CAN showed its willingness to pay any amount, the govern-*
> *ment canceled the permit altogether, asking CAN to hold the*
> *crusade in one of the churches.*
>
> *By Sunday, October 13, when Bonnke arrived in Kano,*
> *the organizers of the rally had bombarded Kano State with [an]*
> *advertisement blitz. The city was literally covered with bills*
> *announcing that "the anointed man of God" is coming to*
> *deliver sinners and unbelievers to Jesus Christ. On state televi-*
> *sion and radio, the announcement was constant and there was*
> *no escape from it. Since until very late, CAN was still thinking*
> *of the Race Course as the venue, all the announcements were*

still mentioning the Race Course as the venue. The Islamic fundamentalists were determined to prevent this at all cost. But in constant touch with the authorities, CAN decided to hold the crusade at Saint Thomas Catholic Church, Sabon Gari.

Fueling the growing tension was the medium of rumour. Friday, October 11, after the afternoon prayers, rumour went round that Bonnke was not just planning a crusade, but was actually leading "an invasion" and would separate Kano from its Islamic roots. It was also alleged that CAN and the visiting evangelist were bent on making some provocative statements about Holy Prophet Mohammed and the Islamic faith. The fundamentalists feared not only an attack on their faith, but were also afraid that some Muslims might actually be converted. To make matters worse was the climate of suspicion that had hung over the city since the Bauchi riots of April. The fundamentalists were preaching that their Muslim brothers were victims of conspiracy, claiming that Muslims suffered more casualties during those riots than Christians.

…Indications that there might be trouble occurred on Saturday, October 12, when some Christians coming for the crusade from other states were attacked at Gamji, a small town between Kano and Zaria. …At about 9 a.m. last Monday, Muslim youths started gathering at the Kofar Mata Eide-ground. There they were addressed by several Islamic teachers. The topic was the upcoming visit of the German evangelist whom speaker after speaker claimed was going to blaspheme Islam.…

At this point Babarinsa goes into detail about the lack of readiness on the part of the police and army for this violence. During their time of hesitation, the rioting continued with many "gory tales of households set ablaze and men and women slaughtered, their bodies dumped in pit latrines. A lot of damage had been done before a reinforcement of anti-riot policemen came from Kaduna, Katsina and Niger states."

Babarinsa continues his tale about thousands seeking refuge in local police stations and military barracks. One station hosted no fewer than 10,000! One Nwoha, an Ibo, explained that he was able to escape from an attack due to his wearing local dress. Those dressed in western fashion, as is the case with many Ibos, were more readily recognized and thus were more readily victimized. Nneka Ukpai, an Ibo lady, appealed to a Muslim family friend who was part of an angry Muslim mob to protect her family. Under such tense circumstances, personal cross-religious friendship not infrequently gives way to the pressure of co-religionists. Her appeal was not heard—her husband and son were killed right before her eyes by her friend's mob.

Since Christians retaliated in this riot, Muslims, of course, also had their victims. Unfortunately, I have not found a national magazine that emphasizes this side of the story. Babarinsa does include the story of one Alhaji Ali, who lived among the non-indigenes in *Sabon Gari*. His house was attacked and he lost four cars to fire. He escaped getting killed "by the skin of his teeth."

This story about Alhaji Ali emphasizes a major difference between this riot and most earlier ones in that Christians and non-indigenes—casual identification of these two usually leads to a distortion of facts and interpretation—mostly Ibos, retaliated. They also burnt buildings and killed Muslims. CAN denied that it had planned this retaliation and insisted it was a spontaneous response from a threatened people. Not everyone accepts this disclaimer.[20]

Karl Maier writes about the reaction of Ibos. As he walked around the scene of the carnage, he saw that "rows of shops had been burned to the ground." He met Ibo traders who had lost everything, shops and houses and, in more than a few cases, relatives. He met a huge, twenty-year-old "muscle-bound" Ibo youth leader named Ndubusi Ikena,

*who admitted to participating in the killing and the torching
of mosques. His aggressive bearing left little doubt that he had.
"They have been treating us like slaves for years," he said of
the Hausas. "When they started attacking us, we carried out
revenge." In response to the calls for peace, Ikene said, the war-
ring gangs had approached each other on the street.... Above
their heads they held sticks and metal bars, as well as green
leaves as symbols of peace. Then, as they came together, they
downed their weapons and began embracing each other. "We
did it because they begged us to stop fighting," he said. "But it
is not finished."*[21]

C. Kano, 1995

The previous sentence is a prophetic statement that would take
only a few years to be fulfilled. On May 30, 1995, my wife and I
drove into Kano. Little did we know that the commotion we ran
into was the beginning of yet another riot. We turned around and,
under police protection, went around the city to the airport. Kano
was about to become the scene of yet more vicious carnage.

The atmosphere in the city had been tense ever since the
beheading of an Ibo trader, Gideon Akaluka, on December 29,
1994. Several stories are making the rounds about him. One is that
Akaluka's wife allegedly used some pages from the Qur'an as toilet
paper for her baby, thus devastatingly desecrating that sacred document. The husband was jailed, supposedly for his own protection.
Another story puts Akaluka in prison for some other reason. While
there, he studied the Qur'an and wrote marginal notes in it. Such
marginal notes have been known to evoke the ire of Muslims for
what they regard as desecration. Still another variation is that
Akaluka himself, while in prison, used the Qur'an as toilet paper,
probably out of desperation. Whatever the exact provocation, a
band of followers of Abubukar Mujahid, a breakaway from El-
Zakzaki's Islamic movement, broke into the jail, beheaded Akaluka

and paraded his head around Kano city. They ended up in front of the Emir's palace. When a representative of the Emir came out to condemn this brutal action, the crowd beat him up.[22] According to Kantiok, the government found that the original accusation was not true, but they did nothing to apprehend the killers.[23] In the meantime, they refused to release his "body and head," fearing this would lead to more violence. It seems to have had the opposite effect.

According to Samuel Uche, Kano CAN Chairman, it is precisely this incident that helped create the atmosphere for the 1995 conflagration.[24] Like most of the others, it took only a spark to set it off, an irrelevant spark that really had nothing to do with any Christian-Muslim issues.

As the story has it, two Hausa women had parked their car in front of an Ibo shop. While they were shopping, two Hausa men burgled the car and stole a bag. The Ibo trader identified the culprits to the ladies, who then reported the incident to the police. The police charged the culprits but released them almost immediately. The two men then picked a fight with the Ibo, who reported them. Other Hausa people in the area saw the fight and immediately took the side of their Hausa brothers, totally disregarding the reason for the fight. There was no way they were going to allow an "*arne*" or "*kaffiri*[25] to beat up a Muslim, regardless of the issue involved.

As usual, the fracas soon spread into the streets throughout the city. I follow the story as reported by Minchakpu. "Muslim fanatics took to the streets killing anybody who could not say [in Arabic]…'There is no God but Allah.'" A woman was riding on the back of a motorcycle when she and her driver ran into a pack of rioters. The driver, a Muslim, was dismissed immediately, but this lady, a Christian, was hit with a stone that broke her skull. An elderly Muslim gentleman rescued her by pulling her away. As she was being pulled to safety, she saw another woman killed right on the same spot. A young Christian boy was chased, caught and slaughtered right on the spot as well.

The rioters then went to St. George's Anglican Church, the church at the centre of the 1982 controversy. Over forty of them, armed with "knives, machetes and other dangerous weapons," forced their way into the church premises, chanting *"Allahu akbar!"*—the familiar Muslim war cry, "God is great!" They called for the head of Canon Gedege, who managed to escape with his family through a back gate. The mob then set the church ablaze.[26]

From there, the mob moved onto other targets. The next one to be burnt was an Ekklesiyar 'Yan'uwan Nijeriya (EYN) church at Brigade, one of those also burnt down back in 1991 during the Bonnke fracas. The pastor had gotten wind of it ahead of time and called for police protection. He was assured that their location was not a target. Alas, only a few hours later…. When the pastor, Audu Dirambi, reported the destruction to the same police officer the next day, he was simply told to report to the government![27]

By now the residents of the *Sabon Gari*, the non-indigene quarters of the city, recognized the need to defend themselves and set up strategic roadblocks to prevent the mob from further penetrating the area. These became the war fronts where many were killed and much property destroyed.

The state government, who put the number of casualties at three, once again downplayed the horror. Military sources gave a figure of "over twenty-three"; CAN, "over sixty"; Murtala Hospital reported "about 200." Muslim leaders are reported to have taken eighty corpses from the hospital for "secret burials."

Then a disagreement set in between the government and CAN over the disposal of the corpses. The government wanted a quick mass burial and be done with it, thus keeping the truth from the public. CAN insisted on identifying the corpses and releasing them to their families. This, of course, would bring the truth into the open. I do not know the outcome of this disagreement.

The government immediately set up an investigation panel with the usual tasks assigned to such bodies.[28] The chairman soon reported seventeen deaths, thus exposing the government's count as false. A tribunal was promised to promptly try the guilty parties. The panel recommended "adequate compensation" for the victims, but experience in this regard is not encouraging.[29] The panel urged prompt action on their recommendations, since "some of such reports in the past had not been implemented." Yes, tell us about that!

In the meantime, posters and handbills continued to be distributed by Muslims, warning Christians to leave Kano immediately or "face harsh reprisals." Minchakpu asks, "How long would this continue in Kano?" He warns that Kano Christians have resolved in the future "to fight back when attacked by Muslim Fundamentalists."[30]

Samuel Uche, the Canon of St. George's Church, expresses this same warning in much stronger and more frightening terms. The patience of Christians in Kano is beginning to run out, he signaled. In his own words, Christians and the residents of *Sabon Gari* in Kano

> *don't rely on the police. They don't rely on the Army. But I must tell you that Sabon Gari is not an easy field to swallow. As small as we are, there is nothing we don't have, but, moreover, we have God. We're ready. This Sabon Gari can face the whole of Kano State and burn Kano State.... But for the fact that we held our youth, eh! They were ready to face Mobile Policemen. They were ready to face soldiers. They were ready to face this people. We only held them; we only told them, "No." Otherwise, if we didn't hold them, man. I don't want to go into details.... But any day they attempt to come into this area, nobody in Kano will be safe. The Emir, the Governor, the police, nobody will be safe. I don't want to tell you how but it will happen. I must tell you that we're prepared.*[31]

These are the most chilling words I have heard or read from a Christian leader so far. It sounds as if the occasional charge by

Muslims that CAN has weapons and a plan are closer to the truth than I, a "semi-outsider," have been prepared to accept. But that's what happens when Nigerian Christians get pushed to the wall too often. The choice for many has moved from cheek-turning to gun-toting.

3. KADUNA SERIES

A. Kafanchan, 1987

I am treating the Kafanchan riot of March 1987 with considerable detail, because the issues involved are illustrative of almost all the problems dividing Christians and Muslims. An additional reason is that it was of such major proportions that President Babangida described it as an attempted civilian coup.

To put it into a larger immediate context, the Kafanchan riot was preceded by the Muslim publication of such provocative documents as "Jesus Is Not the Son of God" and "The Holy Bible Is Not the Word of God." The Christian community of Ahmadu Bello University (ABU) in Zaria reported that the distribution of videos produced by one Ahmed Deedat, a famous Muslim polemicist from South Africa, dwelt on similar anti-Christian themes. The ABU group accused government agencies, such as various state branches of the national television network and the Kaduna International Trade Fair, of aiding in this distribution.[32] Only six weeks prior to the eruption of the riot, documents were circulating that were so inflammatory and provocative that the Plateau State Governor and security organizations had to step in. These were traced to Jama'tul Nasril Islam (JNI), the Muslim counterpart to CAN, and an Indian student dismissed from the Jos ECWA Theological Seminary.[33] Furthermore, the Muslim Circle at Sokoto University wrote a letter to the Director of National Security Services in which the documents were described as "dangerously provocative to Muslims" and that Muslims "normally react to such mischievous plans...sometimes violently."[34] Now we have adherents of both religions reacting negatively, with both appealing to the government. Tensions were so high in both camps that the situation only required a spark to start off the next conflagration. It all started at Kafanchan in southern Kaduna State, where, according to Karl Maier, there is a tradition of riots that goes back to tax revolts in 1922.[35]

The atmosphere at the Kafanchan College of Education was already charged by a programme of MSS that was held a week before the Christian students had their regular annual event. A highlight of the MSS agenda was a film depicting the Dan Fodio *jihad*, "a highly provocative" one, according to the CAN report. However, Christians did not disturb them.

The Christian programme included a speech about the life and work of Christ. The speaker quoted from two Qur'anic passages. These Qur'anic quotations triggered Muslim students who apparently were in the group just waiting for an offence on the part of the preacher. Theirs was a reasonable expectation. The preacher, one Rev. Abubukar Bako, was a convert from Islam who knows the Qur'an and is known for quoting from it. Converting from Islam demotes one to a status somewhat less than a human and strips one of all human rights and dignity. For such a person to quote from the holy book—something Bako was known for doing on his evangelistic campaigns throughout the north—is a doubly unpardonable sin. His very presence was enough to raise Muslim suspicions and hackles.

So, these students were expecting the quotations, probably even hoping for them, ready to throw stones at the speaker. Hajiya Ai'sha Umaru, a female student with a reputation as "trouble lover," "spearheaded the attack on the speaker." She seized the microphone and shouted to the Muslim boys to help her in the attack and threatened that "if the Muslim boys would not help, then the Muslim girls would take up arms and fight for Islam."[36] According to Falola, she claimed that Bako "misquoted and misinterpreted the Qur'an…and he abused the Prophet Muhammad."

Two Muslim school administrators were drawn into it and asked Bako to just apologize, while they pleaded with the Muslim students to allow the Christian meeting to continue. However, both the Muslim students, mostly members of the Fundamentalist Izala group, and the organizers refused their approach. Instead, the Christians demanded that the Muslims be removed from the meeting place. The administration's attempt to forestall violence was fruitless in this volatile situation. A fight ensued and soon escalated into full-blown ruckus, with sixteen students seriously injured and a church burnt along with the school mosque. Bako escaped through a barbwire fence and remains a wanted person by Muslims.

The situation report of the Jema'a branch of CAN has it that several parties reported the college fracas to the local police, but officer Alhaji Omeka

> *made nonsense of all these reports, since he heard it was the Muslim students that were beating the Christian students. Even when the police later arrived at the college...they did not do anything to save the Christian students. They [Christians] had to force open one of the gates...to escape.*

Omeka's claim that the police helped calm the situation on that Friday "is completely false."

The Christian student meeting continued on Saturday in a church in town, where they were again disrupted and attacked. Undaunted, they continued their meeting on Sunday. This time, Muslims attacked them with sticks, clubs, knives and all sorts of weaponry. This attack then spread to other churches in town and nine people ended up killed. CAN slips in the story of the wounded who sought refuge in the police station, but were driven out by the same Alhaji Omeka, a Muslim, who defended himself with the statement, "We are not safe too."

Simmering old hatreds were suddenly revived as the town was turned into a warfront. Muslims, mostly Izala, began to conduct a reign of terror with their weapons and with petrol meant for burning churches. They held up innocent citizens and would destroy their belongings if they were either Christian or belonged to other Muslim sects. Roadblocks made movement unsafe. Some went about destroying parts of the town, including buildings and cars. Stores and other businesses became targets. The major Christian bookshop was looted. The town crowds returned to the college to attack houses and burned twenty cars there. Crowds faced each other with stones. Christians beat two Muslims accused of planning to burn their church. Besides those injured, eleven were reported dead. As in almost all such reported cases, the local police could not cope with this crisis. Calm returned only with the arrival of outside specialist forces. The role of officer Omeka, in blocking all attempts at peace and even preventing the State Governor from seeing the damage inflicted on churches, is highlighted.[37]

Thanks to exaggerated reports by the government radio about Muslims killed in Kafanchan and mosques destroyed, violence spread to other cities in the state. In Funtua, a "systematic and well orchestrated destruction of Christian places of worship and…parsonages and Christian property took place."

At the end of the *jihad*, eight churches "were reduced to rubble." In Kaduna City, the state capital "with a Christian majority," "Muslims attacked with reckless abandon and destroyed 14 churches." The following Sunday, a band of Muslims attacked the Living Faith Church during worship. They came with a supply of petrol/gasoline in order to burn the building along with the worshippers. The situation was saved by the intervention of the military. Thirteen church buildings were either damaged or totally burnt, many of them along with parsonages.

Zaria was worse hit than any other town in Kaduna State. It is a town with many tertiary educational institutions, including the premier northern university, ABU. On Tuesday at 4:30 p.m., news had it that Muslims were meeting at the Central Mosque on the

ABU campus to plan the "destruction of Christianity in Zaria." When CAN reported the meeting to the police, they were told there was "no cause for alarm as he [the police officer in charge] was closely monitoring the situation." Seventy-four churches were either damaged or destroyed, not to talk of Christian homes, businesses and other facilities. I, your writer, have personally seen whole streets left in ugly black ruins. In addition, roads were blocked, cars set ablaze, people harassed and not a few hurt "amidst Muslim songs of victory." Six policemen were guarding St. Andrew's Anglican Church. However, they were withdrawn and "ten minutes later, the church and vicarage were set ablaze." In Samaru, a village suburb of Zaria where ABU is located, all the churches were burnt down along with other Christian properties and the ABU chapel. In Wusasa, a Christian suburb, all the churches were burnt as well some houses, including that of the Gowon family. In all, over 100 churches were destroyed, along with over fifty cars and uncounted other Christian properties.[38] After the violence had come and gone, including in communities not mentioned here, according to various reports, statewide 152 churches and five mosques were destroyed.

The violence spread far beyond the borders of Kaduna State. The people of Katsina, the capital of Katsina State, "unleashed violent attacks on Christians," their churches and businesses. One church was heavily damaged; five were burnt. Kano State was also heavily hit. University properties were destroyed and Christians and Muslims seriously fought each other in the streets. Normal activities in much of the far north ground to a halt, including schools and markets. Traffic between the north and south was reduced to a minimum.[39]

CAN published a news release about this fracas because it felt "the truth of the matter must be told, for in knowing the truth and standing by it, lies our national salvation." It believed that, once they know the truth, "all Nigerians of good will and the government should take concerted action to stem the tide of Muslim religious intolerance." Whether that optimism was realistic is a legitimate question, indeed.

In case the CAN release of 1987 seems one-sided and propagandistic to some readers, I call attention to a report of these events in a press statement by a group of twenty-two ABU lecturers, comprising both Christians and Muslims. That release, appended to the CAN statement as *Appendix F,* is an indication of CAN's attempts to report as objectively as possible. Though the interpretations of this group and that of CAN differ, the facts of these riots are described in even stronger terms by this bi-religious "neutral" group. Hence, *Appendix F* of the CAN release is attached to this book as *Appendix 1.*

The Chief of Wusasa and brother to Yakubu Gowon, Daniel Danlami Gowon, submitted a report to Kaduna State Commission of Enquiry into the Recent Disturbances. Part of Gowon's submission is reproduced and attached to this book as *Appendix 2.* This material shows that CAN's stories of Muslim attacks on Christians are not mere fictitious fabrications. Others tell similar stories. Please turn to this appendix.

B. Zangon-Kataf, 1992

In February 1992, a violent riot took place in Zangon Kataf, once again in Kaduna State. This one was different from all previous riots in that it was started by the mostly rural Kataf people, a mixture of traditionalists and Christians, with Christians in the lead. The target was the Hausa-Fulani Muslim community, the townspeople. I draw most of my information on these riots from two sources—one Christian and the other Muslim—and we will see how "objective" the description of the "bare" facts of the story are.

According to Jega of *Citizen,* a private Muslim magazine, the initial spark—and there always is just a spark that gets the violence going—was provided by an order from Juri Baban Ayok, the

Christian Chairman of the local government. In order to break the alleged monopoly the Hausa settlers had long enjoyed, the local market was directed to relocate. There is some evidence that it was not a purely spontaneous outburst. Some people, including the Christian Chairman, seemed to have foreknowledge of trouble brewing some days earlier. One Alhaji Mohammed Tasiu reported that John Toro, a Christian Kataf and retired army sergeant, told him on February 5 that there would be violence the next day. Ayok himself had told one of his councillors that some ex-servicemen "had threatened to deal with anyone who opposed the relocation of the market." Bestman Tailor was seen packing his supplies a day or two earlier, an indication he might have been aware of something brewing.

The relocation exercise was apparently badly planned and thus quickly evoked resistance on the part of the Hausa traders. The announcement was made on January 30, the very day that bulldozers started working on the new site. The move was to be made in only one week! It is not a pretty story: "There wasn't a single stall or toilet facility at the new market, and pieces of land for traders to erect stalls were first given out on the day of the commissioning itself, February 6."

Furthermore, Ayok had not obtained an approval from the full local council, while the new site was under the direct jurisdiction of the state government and had been designated for a special purpose.

Jega continues,

> Hausa[40] traders in Zango resented the…action and saw in it a political vendetta, especially since the official reason for the relocation was shortage of stalls. They were quick to point out that the new one had not a single stall. The Hausa protest was led by Alhaji Danbala ATK, who was heard on Federal Radio Kaduna's programme…on February 3, urging traders not to move to the new site. On February 5, Danbala obtained an

*injunction from the…court restraining the local council from
relocating the market the next day. The injunction was served
on both the council chairman and the police by ATK himself
on February 6. The police superintendent Audumanian Audu
ignored the order on the grounds that it was irregular, and he
instead ordered his men…to ensure that the new market site
was protected. Mr. Audu had…sent a signal to police headquarters in Kaduna warning that the market relocation could
lead to violence. The policemen at the new market were con-
fused…by the conflict between their orders…. The situation
soon got out of hand and the conflagration ensued.*

The violence started on February 6. Jega's write-up about it
consists mostly of what he learnt from the Cudjoe panel appointed
by the government to check into the matter, not from personal
observation or research.[41] But let us give him our ear.

On the morning of the sixth, armed Kataf youth were on the
road towards Zango. The attack in the town began at nine a.m. On
that day, reported one Dauda Alijyu, John Toro "shot him in the
right eye and then shot dead his two brothers." Hassana Aruwa was
the only survivor of a family of eight. She identified the killers of
her husband and her son respectively as Marcus Jibiro and "one
Sule." Ibrahim Chakakai identified the group that burnt their
house. The group included a pastor and a number of others bearing Christian names. Yunana Zulai Auta said that the looting of her
restaurant was led by her next-door neighbour, Bestman Tailor.
Another, Hussaini Muturba, claimed that his house was attacked
by a group that included his neighbour. They forced their way into
his house and announced, "Today you are dead." They stabbed his
teenage crippled daughter with a knife. These stories are all about
Kataf assailants and Hausa victims.

The role of the police in Zango was questioned. Officer Audi
sent a warning of impending trouble to headquarters when Hausa

people beat up the driver of the grader leveling the new site. In the middle of the bloodshed, some police tried to extract bribes from the victims. When Muturba reported the murder of his family, the police demanded money from him "to buy the paper to record his statement."[42] The man borrowed the money, a measly ten naira, and wrote his report. Afterwards he was taken to retrieve the corpses, but by that time it was dark and they could not be found. Hence, the police locked him up for bringing them false information and "demanded another 2,000 naira to release him!" It's all part of a day's work!

However, the greatest police blunder, according to Jega, was their failure to arrest anyone for several weeks, even after being nudged by the panel and others. They gave various excuses for this failure. They did not want to pre-empt the panel's task of identifying the culprits, they claimed. Furthermore, they feared that doing so would lead to new violence. As it turned out, it was this failure that led to the much greater violence on May 15.

The damage was great. Millions of nairas of vehicles, farms and equipment were destroyed, including thirty-eight cars and nine motorcycles, 133 houses and twenty-six farms. Ninety-five people were killed, while 252 went to the hospital for treatment of wounds. No statistics are available about the wounded treated at home. In distinction from other riots, most of the victims were Hausa Muslims.

Today's Challenge reports that after the first riot, the Emir of Zaria—the one under whose regime the southern Kaduna people were chafing—came to visit the Hausa community of Zango and contributed considerable money to them. He did not bother to call on the representatives of the Kataf. Similarly, state government relief supplies went only to the Hausa; the Katafs were again bypassed. The Emir then called the Kataf leadership to come to his palace in far-way Zaria. They refused to come because he had snubbed them. Realizing his mistake, the Emir then paid the Kataf a visit as well and contributed an equal sum of money to them.[43] Of course, the damage had been done. The attitude of the Emir was clear.

I have covered the first Zangon-Kataf riot mostly with the help of *Citizen*, a magazine with a strong Muslim bias. I am now moving on to the second installment and consciously switch over to Christian sources. You will notice that the tone and direction of the reporting immediately takes on a very different slant. We are going to experience something about the nature of "facts."

The tension of the February riot had not yet dissipated when Muslim youth in Zangon Kataf on May 9 wrote a letter to the Sultan of Sokoto, the official head of the northern Nigerian Muslim community. They threatened to start "the Nigerian Islamic *Jihad* from Zangon Kataf," and promised it would engulf the entire country.[44] Copies were sent to various security and other government agencies, including local authorities. The letter contained a catalogue of "various misdeeds allegedly being meted out" to the local Hausa (Muslim) community by the Katafs. *TC's* report describes both the allegations and the threat as "grave." Unfortunately, I do not have access to this letter.

Various versions exist about the specifics of the resulting riot on May 15. *TC* reports that a mere two days before this riot, busloads of strangers had come to Zango. They were thought to have come from Bauchi and Kano. Some were intercepted in a struggle before they entered the town. During the scuffle, both sides lost four people each. Though the quotation below may not be well organized, its import is clear.

> *TC insists that the actual renewed rioting began with a gang of Hausa youths who fell into a large farm and began to destroy the yams. When Kataf adults came, they had to immediately retreat as they were attacked by well-armed Hausa men who had taken positions everywhere. The police were alerted but could not contain the situation.*

The Katafs sent distress calls to their kith and kin and orga-
nized...for self-defence. This resulted in all-out battle lasting
from about 12 noon of Friday to 1 p.m. on Saturday, May 15-
16. It is alleged that sophisticated weapons, including machine
guns and grenades were used in the fracas. People at Zonkwa,
about forty kilometres away, said they heard the sounds of
artillery fire and saw columns of smoke from the "war zone."

The Hausa community had stockpiled serious weapons of
warfare over time and were sure they could "finish the Katafs
in three days." The indigenes were living in fear as the Hausas
never concealed the fact that they were ready for a show down.
Trenches were said to have been dug in the town which is
exclusively inhabited by Hausas and movement of indigenes
restricted within the town.

...Added to this, there were accusations and counter-accu-
sations alleging destruction of yam farms in the night. One day
before the riots, at least nine Katafs woke up to discover that
their farms had been vandalized. When the following morning
people were seen vandalizing a farm, they provided a clue as to
the people who had been carrying on earlier destruction.

The Hausa community seemed battle ready. It is claimed
that they did not send their children to school that day and those
who work at the Local Government Secretariat were absent that
Friday. Thus, far from being taken unawares, the Hausas were
well armed, ready and confident over victory on the strength of
their arms. It is equally suspected that the delayed arrival of
police was based on the knowledge that the Hausas were prepared
enough to deal with the Katafs and tame them once and for all.[45]

On basis of all the foregoing *TC* materials, it was clear to that
writer that the events of May 15 were no accident but had been
anticipated by the local Hausa people and that they started it. The
anonymous writer continues,

It is not true that they [the Hausa] were rounded up in mosques as no one went for Juma'at prayers that day. But having lost, they now took their casualties to parade in Kaduna to arouse religious sentiments not just against Katafs but all Christians. Thus a purely communal fracas in a village was transformed into a wider religious war covering the whole state, and resulting in the death of many Christians, burning of churches and property....[46]

By the time the actual fracas in the town was over, Zangon Kataf had become a "ghost town. All the Hausas had deserted the place.... Every space was a grave yard and the only buildings standing were mosques."[47]

The reporter in *TC* has begun to notice a pattern to riots that has also become very obvious to me as I move from one riot to the other. The pattern is that

a quarrel arises between Muslims and their neighbours in a remote place. The quarrel results in a clash, which results in deaths on both sides. The Muslims carry their dead bodies and injured ones to the cities where the sight will provoke those of their faith into rage. Consequently a vendetta is unleashed on innocent and unprotected Nigerians.[48]

That's exactly how the riot spread to Kaduna City. The dead Hausa victims and the injured from Zangon Kataf were brought to the city by buses and cars. There they were used to whip up emotions. The government allegedly announced inflated casualty figures. Muslims in Zangon Kataf, they reported, were being killed in cold blood and needed to be revenged. In response, groups of Muslims decided to attack Christians on Sunday. Muslim youths came out "with bows and arrows, cudgels, cutlasses and axes... killing and maiming." They claimed they were on a "mission of revenge on indigenes of Kataf."

And so, on Sunday, May 17, 1992, they attacked Christians in various parts of Kaduna City. The following morning, various church officials were found murdered: Katung, the Zaria CAN Secretary, was "stabbed in the stomach and beat...to death." They "butchered" Bije, an elderly Baptist pastor. They "gouged his eyes and cut through his mouth to his chin. They also burnt down his church, his residence and all the property in it," including two vehicles. Duniyo, an ECWA pastor, "was equally mangled by the mob...in his house. They also cut him deeply across the mouth." Rev. Tacio was killed at home and "dragged out to the street where his body laid for 24 hours.... His car was also burnt and the doors and windows of his house smashed."

Killed along with him in his house were two others. In the meantime, his church was the scene of a mob attack in which at least twenty-five members were killed. The church itself was burnt for the second time, along with the pastorium. Various other churches in the city were burnt and individuals seriously wounded.

It needs telling also that quite a number of Christians who managed to escape their attackers were hidden and protected by Muslims in their houses at great risk to themselves.[49]

The fracas also hit Zaria hard. Sensing danger, many Christians sought refuge in the Federal Prison, thinking it would be a safe haven. Alas, a crowd of Muslims stormed the place, made a hole in the outside wall and set the place ablaze, burning all who could not get out. Those who sought to escape through the hole ran into a mob waiting to finish them off. Staff, prisoners and refugees, with a few exceptions, all died.[50]

The May riot was not only worse than the earlier one, but Mohammed Haruna of *Citizen* judged it to be the most violent of all riots so far.[51] That, in the Nigerian context, is no distinction to be proud of, for it indicates continued escalation to ever-new heights of violence.

So, you have experienced two different views of the story. The "facts" are difficult to determine when people go about their research in a biased way. This gets worse when people are not aware of their bias. The publisher of *Citizen* was sure enough of his line that he declared their reports "were probably the most accurate."[52] Well done and congratulations!

C. Kaduna City, 2000

These stories just won't end. We have now moved into the new millennium and have reached the parameters of this study, but the violence continues. In 1999, the Governor of Zamfara State, a poor and backwater kind of place, brought his state into the national and even international limelight when he announced his intention to adopt the shari'a and its court system in 2000. I will not go into all the details of this controversial development here, as that subject is reserved for a later volume. However, it set into motion a move by many hardcore Muslim states to follow the example.

Among the issues in the resulting hot "debate"—it was more like a contest of screaming among the deaf—were the constitutionality of this move, the comprehensive nature of Islam, the secularity of the nation and whether Christians would be affected or not. Though the governors denied that Christians would be affected, experiences of Christians with shari'a courts under the old order have made them very nervous and suspicious. In addition, there had already been too many examples under the new shari'a dispensation where Christians allegedly were clearly affected.

Not a few non-indigenes left the affected states to avoid renewed violence. Many moved to Jos, the capital of Plateau, considered a Christian state where such a development was thought unlikely. Many others returned to their states of origin. The situation was different for Kaduna, a state largely under Muslim political control but containing a high proportion of indigenous Christians who have no intentions of leaving their homeland. They are determined to slug it out. Kafanchan and Zangon-Kataf are both part of this state.

The Kaduna riots of 2000 represent a new development in that it looks like Christians and Muslims started attacking independently from each other. Both felt provoked and both seem to have been initiators. The fracas ended with an estimated 2000 dead, more than any other except the Maitatsine riots and, possibly, developments in the new Nassarawa State recently cut out from Plateau State. President Obasanjo described it as one of the worst bloodletting exercises in Nigeria since the civil war[53]—a similar thing said of the Zangon-Kataf episode by his predecessor.

The *Newswatch* issue covering the first installment of these riots[54] warned on its cover that "Shari'a will lead to open war," a quote from Archbishop Okogie. That certainly was the case locally and, in fact, beyond. Asaju and Oladipo assert that the riots had their roots in the peaceful anti-shari'a Christian march, on February 21 in Kaduna, organized by CAN. That one had been preceded by another peaceful Christian anti-shari'a demonstration on January 5 in Zonkwa, some miles down the road. The report has it that "hundreds of thousands" of Christians participated in it, most likely a highly inflated figure.[55] The Kaduna demonstration was a response to a pro-shari'a march by Muslims two weeks earlier and some other provocations. Among these was the perceived denial to Christians of channels to have input into the shari'a issue. There was, according to Awowede, an "unwillingness by the Muslims to let the Christians have their say…." Or, as Nosa Igiebor put it, Muslims displayed "total disregard of the feelings and opinion of the Christian community."[56] This was made worse by Christian insistence that they really constitute the majority in Kaduna State. Muslims were going about the city for five days, demanding that shari'a be introduced. In addition, the committee appointed by the House of Assembly to make recommendations on the issue had only Muslim members.[57] When the Governor appointed his own committee, it was not much different. All of these factors put together, along with the Governor's public insistence that shari'a is a must, drove Christians to the wall.[58] The government should have appreciated the peaceful intent of their demonstration and done all it could to protect it. Alas....

Christians had been advised to lock their shops during the event. Over 50,000 Christians, mainly from the southern part of the state, showed up. The event included some activities probably not scheduled by the organizers. In various places, Christian youth were seen "marching and doing exercises" at 5:30 a.m., undoubtedly creating unrest and provoking anger among their Muslim counterparts. The procession moved towards Lugard Hall, the home of the state's House of Assembly, and from there went on to Government House, where they entered after overpowering the security staff.[59] Muslim anger increased along with shouting and threats. While the leaders of the procession were getting ready to see the Governor, a report made the rounds that Muslims had killed one Christian. There was the rumour that provided the spark.

The factual details are murky. According to Awowede, Muslims made the counterclaim that Christians provoked the fighting. He then tries to set the record straight by insisting that actually a group of *almajirai*, children attending Qur'anic schools—always ready for some excitement and easy prey for mischief—had "taunted" Christians, and that the first person to be attacked was an Igbo Christian. In retaliation, two Muslims are said to have been killed—and thus "began the orgy of violence."[60] Of course, facts in such situations are not as important as dangerous rumours.

Panic set in. By 10 a.m., three mosques had been burnt. An attempt to torch St. Joseph's Cathedral was successfully resisted. The mob then turned to looting and ransacking area businesses. In the process, they got hold of liquor, thus further inflaming already aroused passions. Many non-indigenes had their homes burnt. Corpses littered the streets. During the ensuing night, armed indigenous youth groups shouting *"Allahu akbar!"* rampaged through Christian areas. In the Kawo area, reporters saw twenty roasted bodies.

As Muslim mobs tested the religion of people by demanding they recite some Qur'anic verses or else, so Christian groups would release people only if they swore they opposed shari'a. As the day wore on, religious passion was usurped by looters' passion. Some people escaped the clutches of mobs only by giving generous sums of money. Among the rioters arrested were two men who "confessed that they specialized in burning churches and killing pastors. Their blood-stained clothes gave adequate testimony to that."61

By the time President Obasanjo visited Kaduna, he found the city "in ruins."

An important, overtly Christian source of these events is B.E.E. Debki's report to the EYN, the Church of the Brethren in Nigeria, which was reworked into a book as per the church's request. I hardly regard this an objective discussion or portrait; it is marked by too much anger and one-sidedness. Also some of his facts are different from what we have read in the national news-magazines we consulted above. Its virtue is that it represents established Christian opinion, even though not always expressed in the most acceptable English.

As Debki tells the story, while the government of Kaduna State was discussing the shari'a issue, on December 14, 1999, Muslims staged a public demand for its implementation. The House of Assembly appointed a committee comprising both Christians and Muslims, but before long the Muslim chairman, Ibrahim Ali, began a campaign in favour of shari'a, while the opinion of the Christian members was ignored. Debki observed that the pattern of violence in each ward or section of the city was to

> *slay the pastor, sometimes with his family, and set the pas-*
> *torium and the church on fire, before any other operation. As*

a result, hundreds of Christians were killed, many Christian houses destroyed, many churches burnt and a lot of Christian properties worth billions of Naira were destroyed or looted by the hungry Moslem jihadists as they went around with petrol, guns, sword and stones. The jihadists would kill either by gun, sword and a stick, and burn the remains to ashes....

Christian youths began defending themselves with sticks and stones, and before anyone could know what was going on, both sides were involved in the killing and destruction of properties of each side. Thus, where Christians are dominating, they killed more Moslems and destroyed more of their properties. And where the Moslems are dominating, they killed more Christians and destroyed more of Christian properties.[62]

A second crisis developed on May 22, 2000. During the interim, more isolated burnings and destruction of churches took place, including killings of Christians. All the while, Radio Kaduna, a federal institution, encouraged new tensions to build up through one-sided reporting. Apparently they did not take a clue from the Bauchi news blackout that occurred earlier (reported later in this chapter). By early May, Muslims allegedly were planning another war. In preparation, they had transferred their wives and children to Barnawa, a Muslim section of the city.

When Christian youths got wind of these developments, new clashes developed that soon engulfed most of the city. During the interval, both Christian and Muslim youths had been taught the use of guns and were eager to experiment with them. Muslim boys were allegedly given army uniforms and guns. Total confusion set in, since it was now impossible to identify the fake from the genuine. It took the military with armored tanks to bring the violence to an end.

Muslim perpetrators included several groupings of poor people who would do anything for pay. One group comprised unemployed graduates of Qur'anic schools whose "duty," in Debki's words, "is selling of troubles, and can be hired by anyone, including non-Moslems, once one can pay...." In addition, a lot of poor foreigners were employed by the Muslims in these riots, including criminals. Their interest in this excitement was not the low pay, but the looting. The final group consisted of local citizens, some of whom allegedly killed each other during the mayhem to get rid of debts or to cover up secrets.

Minchakpu provides us with some terrible stories of personal tragedies. Father Bello, a recently ordained Roman Catholic priest, came from a Muslim family, but his mother had converted to Christianity. Bello was the only male Christian in the family. As a convert, he was an apostate who had no human right to life, according to Muslim standards. A Muslim mob "dragged him, killed him, tied a rope around his neck and dragged him into a culvert and left him there."

And then there is Minchakpu's story of Mamduh and his wife, Manal. I reproduce their terrible story in its entirety for its full impact.

> *They had been hiding in their home for 36 hours, since riots first broke out in their village against Christians on Friday night. Just before noon on Sunday, the armed rioters managed to break into their house. Mamduh was felled with one blow of a rifle butt, knocked unconscious with blood streaming from his head. Manal quickly grabbed the three boys and squeezed them into a tiny cupboard space behind the stairs. Trembling in fear, they heard furniture being dragged across the floor and out the door. When Manal no longer heard any movements, she ventured out to see part of the house on fire. Mamduh had regained consciousness, but could help little...to douse the flames.*
>
> *It wasn't long until the looters returned, forcing the whole family to scramble under the bed.... One of the*

raiders promised not to harm them, calmly telling Manal to come over to him. Terrified they would attack her, Mamduh came out from under the bed. The attackers forced Mamduh down the stairs. So Manal followed, scooping up the baby in her arms and the other two boys following. "My husband also pled for mercy," she said. "But one of the men beat him on the head...and he fell to the floor. I tried to go to him, but they grabbed me by my hair and dragged me out of the house."

A Muslim neighbour who knew her spotted her, and together with two acquaintances, took charge of her and her children, walking them through the streets to the safety of his own home.... It wasn't till very early the following morning, when she tried to return to her home alone to find her husband, that she learned that, after she left, Mamduh had been shot dead and his body set afire.

Seeing her alone, two Muslim villagers accosted her on the street, threatening to kidnap her unless she signed with her thumbprint a cheque from her husband's account for N50,000 ($14,700). Although she knew such a staggering amount was not in their bank account, she complied. But the moment she turned around, they shot her twice in the back. Her shoulder bone was shattered by the bullets. "But I could still walk," she said, "so I went a very long way before finally I found an ambulance."

"I know who shot my husband," she admitted. "The neighbours saw them do it. I've told the police the names of all three of them." Recently though, she learned one had been released by the police.

"My brothers are helping me," Manal said. "I am so ashamed to keep living off them. But what can I do? I married when I was 15 and I don't know how to read or write."[63]

About a year later, *TC* published some more detailed stories of murders that had taken place during these riots. Laraba Bobai tells how the son of a Muslim neighbour started throwing stones at their house. While they asked him why, suddenly a group of furious and heavily armed Muslims descended on her house. They surrounded the place and "torched it" with her and her children inside. She tried to escape, but Muslims were waiting outside to kill them. One

> *actually sprang forward with a knife intent on killing her. But a gender-sympathetic fellow shot out his arm to shield her from it. By his wound she was saved. A cut on the head inflicted by another wicked one reminds her of that ordeal. Others were not that lucky. Among them were the three women and many children she left behind. All died in a miniature hell. Laraba saw their corpses when she returned. Dead bodies littered the compound. Some, including her husband's, were thrown into the well in the house.*

Hajara Magaji tells how her Muslim neighbours, with whom they apparently had gotten along just fine, called her oldest son and "boldly told him that his end, along with that of all members of his family, had come. Later, their big house was encircled and all exits blocked." There were thirty people in her compound, including many neighbours. Only eight survived the ordeal. She herself was fortunate to have escaped with knife cuts and getting stoned.[64]

The Baptist Seminary in Kawo, a Kaduna suburb, got badly hit during the ruckus. The following is the story there as told by Yusuf Gwadah to Dr. Danny McCain, his former teacher at the University of Jos.

Since it speaks for itself, I include it as Appendix 3 without further comments.

So far, my descriptions of Kaduna 2000 have been based on Christian sources.[65] I now want to show how Muslims describe these same events. I am at a disadvantage here, for Muslim sources at my disposal are fewer. My major source here is the *New Nigerian*— indeed, a Muslim-oriented newspaper, but which always has to temper its preferred orientation because it is owned by the Federal Government. It thus toes the fine line between its preferred stance and political correctness as defined by its political masters. In this way, the *NN* is not free like the previous publications we have consulted. The intention here is not to repeat all the horrible stories of Kaduna 2000, except where the "facts" are reported in a significantly different way from what you have read so far.

I single out the *NN* for two reasons. First, because it is respected especially by the Muslim community and, second, because in subsequent chapters we will read of frequent Christian accusations that *NN* usually supports the Muslim side in situations of conflict, even though it is supported by government money.

Muslims felt let down when Christian members of the State House of Assembly allegedly refused to serve on its adhoc shari'a committee. We have already noted the Christian explanation. Other *NN* stories have it that when the subject was on the agenda of the Kaduna State House of Assembly, the public gallery was full of Christians mobilized by CAN. This intimidated the Christian members of the Assembly and led to their refusal to serve.[66] Ibrahim Ali, the chairman of the committee, explained some of the backroom politicking that took place on both sides. He claimed that he privately was able to exact promises from some Christian members to cooperate. That cooperation did not take the form of membership, but the promise that they would help the committee to ascertain the true feelings of their constituency.[67]

The shari'a issue was not merely a matter for politicians and their committees. When JNI organized a seminar on the issue on February 10-12, 2000, *NN* reported that it was attended by "hundreds of thousands of Muslims and non-Muslims," an assertion supported by a picture that indeed showed a huge crowd.[68] The shari'a was in the air everywhere, provoking intense emotions that rendered the people open to easy and dangerous flare-ups. This situation was further indicated by the fact that the ad hoc committee of the House of Assembly had received over 5000 memoranda. The chairman reported that the people were so "sharply divided" and so "adamant" that it put the committee in a difficult position.[69]

Even though the House of Assembly had not yet reacted to the report of the ad hoc committee, a member of the committee, Muhammad Abubukar, spoke publicly about the issue and decried the heat it had generated. He made it clear that, according to him, Christian opposition to shari'a was based on misunderstanding and ignorance. The entire tone of his presentation, as featured in the *NN*, was one of paternalism and arrogance towards Christians who do not know what they are doing. The fact that this speech was reported in the *NN during* the riots leaves the paper open to charges of recklessly encouraging the continuation of the violence. Throughout the riot and its heated aftermath, the paper kept publishing stories about the progress of the shari'a in other states. One could understand this either as a conscious attempt to keep rubbing salt into the wounds of Christians or as encouraging Muslims by showing that shari'a is on a successful march in other states—or even both!

The *NN* headlines about the riots themselves seem very even-handed in that blame is not apportioned to either religion. It talks about "irate Muslim and Christian youths engaging each other in fierce fighting" and about "skirmishes between Christians and Muslims against the adoption of Shari'a." It presents the reactions of the Christian Deputy Governor, Stephen Shekari, in similarly objective tones as well as the reactions of Christian President Obasanjo.[70]

Since I can hardly improve upon its content, I attach parts of a relevant article by Bala Abdullahi and Kayode Kolade, "Kaduna's Killing Fields,"[71] as Appendix 4.

With Governor Makarfi, a Muslim, abroad for business and medical reasons, Shekari, his Christian deputy, must have been embarrassed by the Christian demonstration for which he had denied permission, suggests Obassa. Later, Saidu Dogo, the Kaduna CAN Secretary, denied that the demonstration was unauthorized.[72] I reproduce the story as it unfolds in the pages of *NN* by quoting from and summarizing relevant sections from Obassa's report and others. It must have been a massive operation, "much bigger than the two held…by pro-shari'a Muslims." Reports Obassa:

> *But the sheer multitude of people that embarked on the demonstration was an indication that…CAN mobilized them from various local government areas in the southern part of Kaduna. It has the resources and logistics to do so. The motive for the demonstration, according to the commissioner of police, was to vent their anger over rumours…that government planned to implement shari'a in the state.*
>
> *With the aim of thwarting any move by the Muslim-dominated House of Assembly to pass any shari'a law, CAN led the youths and women to the seat of power. The youths and women were said to have arrived…in the early hours of Monday and took over the streets…as early as 7 o'clock….*

From the beginning there was an unruly element, but it could be argued that this was provoked by the Christian Deputy Governor by his initial refusal to receive a delegation. Reporter Thomas Adedo reports that there were no security staff at the gate for the leaders to speak to. Then word was received that neither Governor Makarfi nor his Deputy Shekari were in, but the story was not believed. Some youths then scaled the fencing of Government House and opened the gates from within. Once in, the crowd soon overwhelmed the security staff. Some even made their way into the kitchen where they helped themselves in the presence of a frightened staff. They left graffiti on the walls. Shekari, the Deputy Governor and fellow Christian, faced with such mass determination, "reluctantly agreed to address the demonstrators."

Once on the street, force soon overcame the intended peaceful nature of the event. Demonstrators "forced motorists to... stick green leaves to windscreens" to show solidarity with their demands. And then came the test. A rumour was started that a demonstrator had been injured in a scuffle. Tension shot up. Before long, a group of Christian youth began to chase a man, presumably a Muslim, and clubbed him to death. On the other side of the road was another group of youths, armed with clubs and petrol cans, menacingly awaiting their turn. As one reporter put it, "What happened from that point can now only be pieced together from obviously jaundiced accounts of those involved in the tragedy" that unfolded.

As Obassa put it:

> *What appeared to be a peaceful demonstration deteriorated into violence. The youths and women armed themselves with weapons ranging from sticks to iron rods in anticipation of a counter-attack by Muslims. They began to apply these weapons on the unsuspecting members of the public. Right in front of the New Nigerian Newspapers Limited, two cars were destroyed and an old man clubbed to death while the other man, [was] beaten unconscious. Soon afterwards, three people were killed near the market. The angry youths were joined by hoodlums spreading the carnage.*
>
> *Eyewitnesses pointed out that the fact that when Muslims were demonstrating over the need for sharia to be implemented, no harm was caused to any Christian. But that was because Christians chose not to confront them.*

Thomas Adedo paints a different scenario. He claims that the original challenge to the Christians was that Muslim youths had barricaded their route and were having their own pro-shari'a demonstration. Christians had entered the city without weapons at hand, but when they met Muslim opposition, they grabbed whatever they could—sticks and stones, clubs, rods—but these were no match for weapons wielded by the Muslims. Many Christians were injured and rushed to a hospital.

Adedo tells how Muslim youths were "going from house to house, identifying Christians, killing and maiming them and their properties destroyed." They carried out similar rampages in other parts of the city. He also reports that Muslims were seen with professional military guns, a claim corroborated by another reporter, Isaiah Abraham, who tells of a military officer who saw "bandits" with weapons "more sophisticated than those given to the soldiers sent to arrest the unrest."

The Christian demonstration in the city was said to be hijacked by hoodlums, an observation overheard with practically every riot ever held in Nigeria. As always, so this time these hoodlums saw to it that the demonstration "degenerated into full-scale confrontation between Christians and Muslims." Throughout the city, "groups of rampaging youths held people hostage, killing, maiming, burning people and houses, shops and vehicles."

One anonymous *NN* writer describes the riot as "one of the darkest episodes in the history of religious conflicts in this country. The destruction was horrendous, as was the senselessness of the rampage...."

It was a "struggle against reason," and said to demonstrate the truth of Martin Luther's dictum that "Reason is the greatest enemy of faith." "All in the name of God?" was the incredulous query of Malam Yahaya Ango, a trader whose shop was torched. One Celestine Ibekwe, probably an Ibo Christian trader, declared, "Those who organized the procession should have realized it was always going to lead to violence."[73] And violence it was, so destructive that the final result almost goes beyond human imagination. Onimisi Alao wrote a report on the devastation after he took a tour around the entire city. It is attached to this chapter as Appendix 5 and is a definite challenge to your tear ducts.

The Acting Governor carefully followed the script of established post-riot ritual in Nigeria by promising that those responsible for the illegal Christian demonstration and other crimes would be apprehended. Another regular part of the ritual he followed was to appoint a five-member commission to investigate, amongst other issues, the immediate and remote causes of the riots and the culprits. The commission was an unusually fair mix of Christians and Muslims. Shekari assured the public that arrests had already been made.

Obassa faults various parties, especially authorities, for not being up to the challenge presented by the situation. He criticizes the police for their "belated arrival," a familiar refrain, and for only trying to contain the mayhem without making any arrests. He reports that people critique Shekari for not acting "quickly and decisively." He especially blames Governor Makarfi for "running with the hounds and the hare at the same time." He should have called the "spade by its name and stop postponing the evil day." Politicians are warned to "stop dabbling into matters that would balkanise the country." Contrary to earlier sections in his report, Obassa refers to those who disagree with each other over shari'a as "fanatics."

There are no precise statistics as to the number of dead, maimed or wounded. Debki reports that "thousands of people were massacred," though his lists fall far short of that huge number. Over two hundred churches were said to have been destroyed during the fracases along with 105 mosques and nearly 9000 houses.[74] These bare statistics, horrible as they are, do not cover the terrible cost in dislocation and severe mistrust that developed in the community.

With both religions advocating peace, Obassa asks about the "cause of the intolerance Christians and Muslims tend to demonstrate at the slightest provocation." It is a good question, but he fails to provide the answer. His calling those who disagree with each other over shari'a "fanatics" is merely a diversionary tactic that places him squarely in the company of those he accuses of failing to call the spade by its name.

Umar Sanda presents us with an interesting background study of the CAN demonstration. He analyses the possible reasons for staging it, as well as the pre-riot wrangling by CAN leaders that took place behind the scenes. Since I could not possibly summarize the major points of Sanda's article adequately, I am attaching most of this article to this volume as Appendix 6. It is a responsible and objective article that does *NN* credit.

Nigerian riots usually are not contained to their original community. This one was no exception. Both *NN* and various issues of *Newswatch* report on the spread of violence to other parts of the state and beyond, even in the deep south, far away from the Muslim world. As to events within the state, there is the story of the Emir of Zaria stopping "young hoodlums" from attacking shops in Zaria. Before it was nipped in the bud, people were already running to the safety of police and military establishments. As always, reports could vary. According to one report, sixty-five people were killed in Kachia, while an *NN* report puts it at ninety. Reports on violence in Kafanchan also circulated.[75] *Newswatch* tells of Musa Bulus in Rigassa, who found his aged father's corpse on the street. "He had been slaughtered and cut into small bits and pieces. His rickety bicycle was put on his corpse and burnt." He recognized the body only because of the rosary "which miraculously escaped the fire." He himself was captured and brought to a mosque to be killed, but, after being stripped of watch and shirt, managed to escape. This same article goes into great detail about the economic losses people in both Kaduna City and in outlying areas incurred in this riot. Absolutely devastating.[76]

Beyond Kaduna State borders, in Kano City tensions rose high. On the Thursday after the Kaduna riots, a "stampede" broke out that led to the closure of business activities. It was serious enough that undisclosed security measures were taken to pre-empt an outbreak and the government warned hoodlums not to take advantage of the atmosphere. This report also contains a surprising admission that probably just slipped past the final editor. The tension rose, the report reads, "since the eruption of the sectarian strike in Kaduna last Monday by Muslims…for the adoption of shari'a."

In Niger State, the threat of an attack on Christians by Muslim youths caused the Governor to meet with Christian leaders to allay their fears. Some Christians had already started locking up their shops and heading for security. The Governor, a staunch pro-shar-i'a Muslim, pleaded with Christians, mostly Ibos, to pursue their business as usual and promised to search out those who sought to profit from the confusion.[77]

Tension in the largely Christian state of Taraba rose when the Muslim Brothers pronounced the death sentence on Okenna Nduka for allegedly desecrating the name of Muhammad. They threatened chaos if the government did not take action. He was promptly arrested "for his own protection." Both in Plateau State and Abuja, public preaching was banned. All these events were fall-out of Kaduna 2000.[78]

As to far southern states, in Umahia, twenty-nine people met their death; two died in Owerri. In these towns, people took revenge by turning on local Muslims for the death of their relatives in Kaduna.

If some of you readers have a hard time believing all these stories, you are in good company. Even President Obasanjo—an army officer during the Nigerian civil war, who must have seen unend-ing war atrocities—upon seeing the ruined city of Kaduna, said, "I could not believe that Nigerians were capable of such barbarism against one another." He continued,

> *The devastation was so massive, it seemed as though Kaduna had overnight been turned into a battlefield. My visit con-firmed…all the reports I had been getting—the mindless killings and maimings, the wanton destruction of property, the fear and uncertainty on the faces of those who survived the carnage, and the pervasive mutual suspicion.*

He expressed astonishment that people who had been good neighbours for decades suddenly "turned on them and massacred them."[79]

4. KATSINA, 1991

The Katsina riot was one of Muslims versus the government. Such riots are not the primary focus of this study. However, here again the issue of secularism lurks just around the corner. As we will see in later volumes, that issue is directly related to our main topic.

It was in April 1991, that Yakubu Yahaya—according to some, a leader of the Muslim Shi'ite sect[80]—defied the Christian State Governor, John Madaki.[81]. The situation soon turned into chaos as buildings and cars were set ablaze. Numerous followers had been brought into the city to support Yahaya. The spark that triggered it was an article in *Fun Times*, a publication of *Daily Times*, that allegedly insulted both Christ[82] and Mohammed by claiming that both had relations with "women of easy virtue.[83] An important consideration here was that the Federal Government owns these papers. Thus the government was accused of endorsing an anti-Muslim attack. It was seen as only one example of the government's generally pro-Christian and anti-Muslim stance.

As Yahaya explains, the reason for the anger at this provocation was that it was part of a long series of insults on the part of various people: "The Prophet Muhammad has been abused too many times in this country." Yahaya gives a number of examples, including one by the prominent late Yoruba politician Awolowo. "We cannot tolerate these abuses," Yahaya asserted.[84]

And so his group first went to the sales office of *Daily Times*, where the offending magazine was stored. They took all the copies of the magazine outside and burnt them. He explains,

> *While doing that, we did not touch any of the staff of Daily Times nor did we insult anybody. We burnt the publications in order to express our displeasure with the Daily Times for*

> *putting up two of our prophets to ridicule. We know that the*
> *punishment of whoever ridicules our prophet is death, but we*
> *could not carry out this sentence because we did not know the*
> *actual person who was responsible for the act. This was why*
> *we had to punish the Company with the hope that our action*
> *will serve as deterrent to others.*

Subsequently, Yahaya went to the mosque to appeal to fellow Muslims to join him in a further protest against the paper's blasphemy. He reminded them that this demonstration was meant to be "peaceful and orderly" and that he would "not hesitate to remove any unruly person from our midst."

Then the police accosted the procession and fired teargas. Confusion set in and people ran helter-skelter. Several government buildings and cars were set afire. Many of the 161 people arrested were imprisoned. When the first ones completed their sentences and were released, members of the Islamic movement from other places came to rejoice with them. Again, the police fired teargas and arrested over 250 of them! Two people died.

Without seeking to defend Yahaya and his crowd, I do wish to point out that government authorities, especially the Nigerian police, have a bad record of handling protests and have more than once made them worse. This becomes clear not only from the complaints of both Christians and Muslims in the aftermath of other riots, but also from the report on police reaction to the Maitatsine riots that was published by the National Institute for Policy and Strategic Studies (NIPSS) in Kuru.[85] Falola feels that Colonel John Madaki, the Christian military governor of this Muslim state, misunderstood the intentions of Yahaya's group to overthrow the government. By acting on this suspicion, he turned the event into a major crisis, probably to the liking of Yahaya and his boss, El-Zakzaki.

The State Government, headed as it was by a Christian military governor, had good reason for being nervous about this demonstration. Yahaya had previously engaged in some pretty radical actions that led to imprisonment. At another time, he gathered a crowd of 1000 or more angry young men to free a member of their group from a court by chasing the judge away. He was also credited with a similar incident elsewhere in the state. Governor Madaki publicly threatened to deal with Yahaya, declaring "I swear to Almighty God in heaven, if he causes trouble again we will take him to the Polo Ground and kill him publicly."[86] In common with most members of the Nigerian Muslim community, Yahaya was sure that this Christian governor was participating in the alleged Federal Government's campaign through CAN to spread Christianity, including secularism, throughout the country. The governor's angry outburst only served to prove the point.

The course of the entire event took some days and involved the importation of 2000 more followers into the city, as well as the involvement of El-Zakzaki himself. The town was slowly worked into a frenzy, with all the parties up in arms and working towards a conflagration. Accusations about abuse of office went back and forth. Newspapers produced their expected editorials. Falola wrote an admirable and revealing report on the entire flow of events that gives a good feeling of the brinkmanship all parties engaged in. Fortunately, Yahaya targeted only government establishments, not private properties or individuals, thus preventing the bloodshed associated with so many riots. Three police were killed and thirty-seven people wounded; various government buildings were destroyed along with five cars.

The police were unusually effective in containing the situation. Many, excluding Yahaya, were arrested, but Yahaya later surrendered himself along with a hundred followers and was jailed. Falola comments that he was "the first leader of a religious riot to be tried and jailed." The end of this episode spelled by no means the end of the movement's provocative stance.[87] We will hear more about Yahaya and his people in following volumes.

5. BAUCHI SERIES

A. Tafawa Balewa, 1991

Bauchi state has experienced a number of riots: 1991, 1995 and 2001. The 1991 riot began when a Christian butcher, a member of the Sayawa ethnic group in the Tafawa Balewa Local Government area, sold meat to a Muslim. Whether it was beef slaughtered by a non-Muslim or whether it was pork, it is impossible to say at this point. In either case, the meat would have been *haram*, or non-*kosher*, to a Muslim. At any rate, the meat itself was not the real provocation; it was merely the spark.

The offended Muslim purchaser, upon discovering the problem, was said to have slashed the seller's arm with a knife. Other Christian butchers came to his rescue, but they, in turn, were overcome by a crowd of Muslims. Other reports have it that when the seller refused to take the meat back, the customer killed him. Fellow butchers in the vicinity, both Christians and Muslims, then killed the customer. Whichever scenario was the case, the fracas escalated and moved to the town. Four days of riots produced over 200 dead and even more injured. Thousands of Christians took refuge in neighbouring states, especially Plateau State. Houses, hotels, shops and some twenty churches were burnt.[88]

Not only did the riot spread to many villages but also to Bauchi City, the state capital. In fact, that is where the greatest material damage occurred. In reaction to the Tafawa Balewa violence, Muslim mobs in the city took to the streets, thousands ransacking everything Christian in sight. Five hundred houses were set on fire, at least fifteen hotels went up in flames, and the same happened to twenty churches along Hospital Road. All mission properties received similar treatment as did the offices and properties of the Christian Pilgrims Board, a government agency. All non-native sections of the city were engulfed. *Newswatch* reports that, though official figures put the death toll at eighty, the mortuaries reported closer to 500. When the city collected corpses strewn along the streets and buried them in mass graves to avoid disease, people had become so hardened that they stood by as the bodies were collected and loaded onto trucks.

One man tells how his brother, Johnson, burned to death.

> *There was smoke everywhere. I ran to the shop. I saw Johnson. He was still inside.... He was trying to get out. But they did not allow him.... One of them with a long dagger was wielding it before him. Other people used long sticks to push him back into the fire.... The whole shop was burning and falling down on him.*[89]

As to the effectiveness and reactions of the security organizations, Falola reports that "the police lost control"—a familiar story. While the riots continued unhindered and more Muslims "flooded into the city," the police, somewhat understandably, spent their time protecting their own families. And so the fracas continued without security resistance for three days. Even a dusk-to-dawn curfew did little to turn the tide. The Federal Government sent in the army, but mob resistance to it ended up in many more deaths and "hundreds more people...arrested." Eventually, many were accused falsely of participating. Falola concludes that "the state itself became a dispenser of brutal violence."[90]

B. Tafawa Balewa, 1994

Three years later, nothing had yet been done to implement the recommendations of the committee assigned to study the causes of the 1991 riot. The state administrator in 1994, a Christian, described the issue as very delicate. For sure! Neither had the promised N25 million compensation package been distributed amongst the victims.[91] When this Christian governor began to show signs of supporting the Sayawa by appointing one of their members to the state cabinet, the former was quickly replaced by Rasheed Raj, a Muslim. To safeguard his appointment, Governor

Raj quickly dropped this Christian commissioner and replaced him with a Muslim, Alhaji Ibrahim,[92] a resident of Tafawa Balewa. The Sayawa people thus lost two powerful allies.

The Tafawa Balewa Council decided to welcome the above Alhaji Ibrahim to his new position with a reception. After all, should they not have been proud of such an appointment of one of their own? Never mind that he replaced a local Sayawa. Adding insult to injury, the council staff and workers were forced to donate to the event. The wives and sisters of these workers objected to this compulsory payment to welcome one they considered a usurper and a sworn enemy of their people, who had publicly opposed their deepest aspirations. To be forced to welcome, at their expense, this man who replaced a son of the Sayawa was about as insulting as it can get. They organized a peaceful protest against the reception.

Salisu Shehu, a Hausa Fulani from Tafawa Balewa and lecturer at Bayero University, Kano, provided some more details via Osa Director. The appointment itself, let alone the reception and the way it was to be funded by the Sayawa, brought the local temperature to a boil. Shehu noted that "hundreds and thousands of people started trooping to Tafawa Balewa" for a reception. Apparently, large crowds planned to avail themselves to this free largesse. However, "they discovered to their amazement that all roads…were blocked with stones and trees to such extent that there was no way any person or vehicle would go into Tafawa Balewa…."

It was this action that led to the postponement of the reception.

When it was postponed, the Sayawas were in the mood to celebrate their victory, according to Shehu. They proceeded to the homes of non-Sayawas living in the community, mostly Muslims, and "started killing and burning their houses." This "orgy of violence," Shehu reported, "lasted for almost one week with grim and frightening statistics of losses and destruction in terms of lives and property." At the end, he counted fifty-four villages burnt and "thousands of people were killed."

The violence seems to have been premeditated. Osa Director relays the sad story of Joel Dogo, a Sayawa Christian. On July 1, 1995, Joel was socializing in his compound with family and neighbours, when another neighbour—a female Fulani Muslim seller of *fura* and *nono,* traditional dairy products—walked into the compound "quivering." She "murmured" to the family that the Hausa-Fulani intended to "unleash violence and destruction on the Christian Sayawa…."

"She told us to flee for our lives before we are killed," Dogo recounts. As he tells the story,

> *We began to run blindly without any specific destination in mind. As we were all running, some Hausa-Fulani, including Ahmadu Musa, called Andrans and Haruna that he wanted to talk to them. With him were Mai Jonka, Yunusa Mai Angwar, Isa Barde, Umaru Musa, Sarkin Noma Sambo and Jibril Barde. At this stage, I decided to make a detour. And I heard Umaru Musa instructing them to pursue and catch me. But I ran into the bush and they could not trace me….*

In Director's words, "What happened thereafter was a nightmare and sheer horror." Dogo managed to climb into a tree. Hidden in its foliage, he watched the bloody proceedings of murder as his friends, neighbours and wife, along with his four children, were slaughtered like rams.

> *Esther, Andran's wife…boldly accused her assailants of treachery and mindless viciousness. "So you can kill people you have lived with from childhood till this day," she…asked her captors. This "affront" was said to have irritated…them. In anger, she was the first to be killed. One after the other the captured Sayawa were slaughtered. The most traumatizing moment came, as Dogo recalled, "when they moved near my wife. In rage I almost fell from the tree…but I managed to*

*cling onto the…tree. When they finished, they shook all the
dead bodies to be sure they are properly dead.*

Colonel Yohanna Madaki, a one-time military governor who
was sacked because he dared take on the Muslim Emir of Muri,
served as the Sayawas' lawyer. He passed on many tales related to
him by his clients. Much of the burning and murdering on the part
of Muslim youth was done in the presence of their elders, according to the testimony of Patrick Tapgun, the Christian Chief
Superintendent of Police for the area. In Madaki's words,

> *This unprovoked attack…resulted into a civil disturbance
> of unprecedented magnitude. In the process, many…were mas-
> sacred in their tens of hundreds, including children, women
> and the aged. More than 1000 lost their houses to fire….*
>
> *In a village called Bununu…which is not inhabited by
> the Sayawas, 22 children…between the ages of 11-16 years
> were…hacked to death…. This is beside the fact that five of
> the family…of one Mr. Joel and four others…in his presence
> were killed.*[93]

The story is told of the burning of the house of Bukata Adamu,
a former Sayawa state commissioner. Though the Sayawa claim that
the place was burnt by Muslims, Salisu Shehu insisted that the Sayawa
burnt it. Even though it was owned by a Christian indigene, they
burnt it because the actual resident was a non-Sayawa Muslim judge
whom they wanted to kill. In addition, the furniture in it belonged to
the hated local government. It would have been impossible for the
Muslims to have set the house on fire, given the fact that it was located
right next to security and police facilities—how could they evade all
these? The difference in explanations from that of Christians here is
interesting, but for that, you will need to turn to Volume Three.

Various Christians presented their versions. Minchakpu's version is as follows:

> *The Muslims set the Tafawa Balewa Central Market ablaze, burnt down the house of the late Bukata Adamu, who lost his relations in the 1991 crisis, and proceeded to destroy and set ablaze 30 Sayawa villages. The aftermath of the actions of the Muslims, was the killing of over two hundred persons, destruction and setting ablaze of 77 churches, and destruction of property worth millions of naira.*
>
> *The lives of those even within the sacred places of worship could not be anything worthy to the Muslims. About 36 women and children that had taken refuge at a church… in…Gungu Zango, were butchered to death by the Muslims. The women even had their bellies ripped open.*[94]

Yakubu Dogara, "a Christian Sayawa and member of Legal Option, a pro-democracy and human rights group based in Abuja," reported that thirty Sayawa villages were burnt down as were eight villages belonging either to Hausa-Fulani or to Jarawa—a total of thirty-eight villages. A local COCIN pastor, Iliya Mailafiya, added that 146 Sayawas were killed and seventy-seven churches burnt.

There were thus some significant disagreements and even contradictions between the Christian and Muslim reports, the sharpest of which concerned who actually started the violence. Director comments that while Shehu gave a list of the fifty-four villages, he did not mention the name of a single individual killed. Shehu disagreed with Dogara's report and argued that nine of the burnt villages claimed by the Sayawas actually belonged to either Hausa-Fulani or Jarawa Muslims. Simple calculation will demonstrate that the numbers do not tally properly, but the point of great destruction is amply demonstrated.

There was also another difference in the way Shehu and Christians reported on the dead. While the former claimed that the Sayawas killed "thousands of people," he did not name even one.

The Sayawas, according to Director, "graphically detailed how most of their kith and kin were killed." According to them, but in Director's words, twenty-two Sayawa students of Government Secondary School, Bununu, were reported trapped in the death zone on their way home and slaughtered by the Hausa-Fulani and Jarawa. At a village called Gungu-Zango, between eighteen and thirty Sayawa women, some of them pregnant, were allegedly slaughtered in a COCIN church building. Dogara supplied the names of all 146 victims in his paper.

Though Director's article was written many months later, the area remained inundated at that time with security people, soldiers and police. Soldiers ran road checkpoints; armoured cars were positioned all around the town. All of this was to indicate that the government intended to deal "ruthlessly with the feuding groups." "Fear, tension and insecurity" still marked the atmosphere.

Unlike the riots of 1991, this one did not spill over into Bauchi city. Director commented that it seemed as if these riots were played out on some other planet, for the rest of the world heard nothing about these developments. He called it "Nigeria's Hidden War." This difference is said to be the direct result of decisions on the part of both Federal and State governments, which decided together to curtail information over the media to prevent its spread as in other riots. In addition, the State government decided not to transfer the victims to Bauchi so as not to rile up its citizens. Medical people were transferred from Bauchi to treat people locally. Thus, "restless religious fundamentalists and undesirable elements in Bauchi town who could have capitalized on the situation to wreak havoc were shielded...." In view of the potential spread of violence, I agree that keeping it hidden was the right decision and I dislike Director's statement that "the junta tries to cover up the bloodbath in Bauchi state." True, it was a cover-up—but a legitimate one, necessary even—though it undoubtedly also was to protect the reputation of Islam. It appears that Director would rather have his magazine and himself profit from the free flow of information, even if it should lead to widespread killing. The media not only report the news; they also influence and even create. The authorities were wise in preventing that, even at the expense of the idol of unrestricted information.

C. Tafawa Balewa, 2000 and Beyond

As we move to the parameters of this study, I cannot refrain from a peek across millennial boundaries. Throughout the period of 2000-2002, this war continued to brew. New spats occurred on an almost regular basis, with nothing apparently solved. In fact, Minchakpu writes that the clashes "have continued unabated for several years." Though it is possible to identify various riots and battles along the way, it is really one prolonged war. In October, 2002, Minchakpu reports more than 200 Christians were killed.[95]

It should be obvious by now that even just getting the basic facts is nigh impossible. Fact, fancy and interpretation are so woven together that unraveling them has become more than a challenge! Going further would lead us into "pure" interpretation, which is the topic for the next two volumes.

6. POTISKUM, 1994

We are not even close to exhausting the list of riots! Another one is that of Potiskum on September 4, 1994. I judge it best to let the editor of *TC*, Obed Minchakpu, report his findings in his own words:

> *Muslim fanatics have again struck! This time setting ablaze nine churches, killing three persons and destroying properties estimated at over 15 million naira.*
> *…Sunday at about 11:00 a.m., the Muslim fanatics numbering over 5,000, and chanting "Allahu Akbar!" poured out to the streets, looking for prominent Christians marked for elimination.*

The fanatics marched to the police station looking for the Division Police Officer (DPO), Mr. Yohanna Dennise, a Christian, to kill him so as to pave way for carrying out their plans to attacking Christians unhindered.

Unfortunately for them, the DPO was not at the station. And so, they went wild, destroying glass louvers of the windows in the station and other properties.

The fanatics then moved to the palace, where the Emir Alhaji Abali Muhammadu, addressed them before they proceeded to the house of the Chairman of [the] local Government Council, Baba Dafa, where he addressed them.

The fanatics then moved to the First Baptist Church, where they set it ablaze. Before the arrival at the church, some elders, on sensing the tense atmosphere, had reported the matter to the Emir, urging him to intervene, but the Emir had assured them that nothing would happen.

It was just minutes after the encounter that the fanatics set the church ablaze. The same elders ran back to the Emir to report what was going on, only to be told that the Emir they had met not more than ten minutes earlier had gone to the farm.

The fanatics, armed with knives, machetes, dane guns and tins of petrol, destroyed the pastorium of [the] church, its library and properties estimated at millions of naira.

From there, the fanatics moved to ECWA Church. They set ablaze the church, the pastorium, and office of the ECWA Rural Development. The fence around the premises was also pulled down.

Furthermore, the fanatics killed Pastor Yahaya Tsalibi, who was conducting a communion service. Another member, Ezra Turaki, was also stabbed to death.

At the church, 11 motor vehicles were set on fire, while seven motorcycles and 26 bicycles were set ablaze. This does not include properties estimated at millions of naira that were destroyed.

The fanatics also set ablaze the following churches: St. Peter's Anglican, EYN, Deeper Life Bible Church, Assembly of God, COCIN, St. Luke's, and Cherubim and Seraphim Church, where one J.O. Osuji was stabbed and later died at a hospital.

This destruction was carried out for three hours without police intervention. Police Area Commander, Alhaji Hassan Mashinyi and the Divisional Crime Officer, who are both Muslims, were earlier said to have conspired and lured the DPO into going into hiding, while the fanatics had a field day in carrying out their destructive mission.

The Officers involved in the conspiracy that led to non-police intervention, told the committee of inquiry that they advised the DPO to go into hiding, because the fanatics were looking for him to kill him. They also added that they instructed the Mobile Police Unit stationed outside the town, not to intervene until things got out of hand.

All these lapses and conspiracies on the part of the two police officers provided the opportunity for the fanatics to carry out massive destruction of churches without hindrance. The Council Chairman and the Emir of Fika were also reported not to have done anything to bring the situation under control.

Reports show that the fanatics, under the leadership of a Koranic Malam by the name Malam Hassan Adamu, carried out the mayhem under the pretext of fighting the cause of Islam.[96]

CAN reacted in a number of ways. It decided not to co-operate with the State government's investigation proceedings. It would neither produce witnesses nor submit any memoranda. It did call on the government for thorough investigation and severe punishment of the perpetrators. It warned all Christians not to depend on the government for their security, since the latter had been "actively involved" in these attacks. Christians should prepare to defend themselves. It also wrote a strong letter to the Head of State, Sani Abacha,[97] the text of which I do not possess.

7. PLATEAU SERIES

A. Jos, 1994

And then there was the case of Jos in 1994. Trying to distinguish itself from other northern cities, Jos has long paraded itself as the capital of the State of Peace. For decades, indigenes have lived comparatively peacefully with large groups of non-indigenous Muslim northerners. That situation was put in jeopardy in April 1994. A peaceful demonstration of indigenous people, comprising of Christians and traditionalists, was followed a few days later by a violent riot on the part of so-called "*Jasawa.*" These were Hausa-Fulani Muslim settlers from Bauchi State, just to the north of Plateau State, who had moved to Jos earlier in the century.

During the early colonial period, Jos was placed under the rule of the Muslim Emir of Bauchi. That Emir appointed a Hausa man Chief of Jos. In 1926, the Jos area was separated from Bauchi, also by the colonialists, and the chieftaincy returned to the indigenous people. In 1987, a Hausa Muslim politician, Alhaji Saleh Hassan, reportedly called upon *Jasawa* youths to recover the chieftaincy of Jos as their right. This call set into motion a set of dynamics that reached its climax in 1994 with the appointment of a *Jasawa* member as Chairman of the Jos North Local Government by the Muslim military administrator of Plateau State. Strong, though non-violent, protests on the part of the indigenes prompted the suspension of the appointment. A few days later, the suspension order led to a violent riot initiated by the

Jasawa. They made havoc of the town and caused significant burning, looting and killing. Only by police and military efforts was "peace" restored, but the tension remained. Neither group gave up its claim.[98]

B. Jos and Plateau State, 2001 and Beyond

On September 7, 2001, a few weeks after my wife and I had completed an extended stay there, Jos erupted once again. A number of incidents contributed to this situation. As in 1994, a Muslim, one Alhaji Mohammed Muktar Usman, was appointed Jos North Chairman as well as Co-ordinator of the National Poverty Eradication programme. The appointment was once again unacceptable to the indigenes, who regarded Usman as a settler.[99] Another part of the story is that of a Christian woman who allegedly passed right through a crowd of Muslim worshippers who had spilled over from the mosque onto the street, as is the custom on Fridays. Muslim vigilantes beat her up for her audacity. Christians retaliated by burning the mosque. The atmosphere was further heated up by pamphlets distributed by the *Jasawa* in which they continued to claim Jos as theirs. All of these factors prepared the city for yet another round of violence. "Weapons were surprisingly and freely used." Both lives and properties were lost[100] with churches and mosques especially bearing the brunt of the anger.

I have in my files many e-mail reports about this conflagration from my two sons, who were caught in this frenzy, and from both Nigerian and expatriate friends. The following are excerpts of e-mails from a Nigerian Christian whose identity I need to protect.[101]

> *The trouble started after the Muslim usual Friday prayers. They rose from their prayers and began attacking innocent unsuspecting people on the road. They were killing, looting and burning houses and businesses along their way. For the Muslims to come to Jos, a Christian city, and kill a Pastor,*

an ongoing unending nation-wide revenge and counter revenge is imminent.

While the above describes Muslim violence, the next day he described Christian revenge against Muslims. These Christians were

ransacking cars and killing anyone suspected to be Muslim. They said they were tired of being killed over and over by Muslims. They were determined to revenge the present and the past killings inflicted on them by Muslims. If you wore the traditional dress (usually Hausa's), you're toast. I saw between 15 and 20 men killed and burnt. About two and a half dozen cars/trucks were also burnt. It is the most dangerous, life threatening thing I ever experienced.[102]

Plateau State has not been able to restore its former quiet atmosphere at the time of writing this paragraph in 2003. The previous riots in response to government actions destroyed the thin fabric of peace between Christians and Muslims in the state. The succeeding riots and violence were the result of the destruction of that fabric and have now taken on a more openly religious character. The state's reputation as the "home of peace and tourism" is fast being replaced, according to Africa historian Wiebe Boer, by one as the "home of pieces and terrorism."[103]

In May, 2002, more killings took place in Jos between the two religions. The fatality figures in one report range from twenty to fifty.[104]

The violence could not be contained in Jos. There has been widespread violence in various localities in Plateau State, but there has been a concentration of it in the Langtang-Wase area. Minchakpu reports violence in Wase Local Government area during July 2002. Some 500 persons died in riots between Christians and Muslims, a figure that grew to "more than 5000," according to Selcan Miner, a prominent clergyman, businessman and politician in the state. The estimate of more than 10,000 persons displaced subsequently grew to "more than 100,000," according to Miner. And while Minchakpu reports the destruction of "more than ten Christian communities," Miner puts that figure at eighty-eight. In view of the entire population of the area standing at 102,491, Miner's figure of displaced persons appears inflated.[105]

8. BORNO-MAIDUGURI, 1998

Under the heading, "Tension between Christians and Muslims Increase in Borno State," we are informed in 1998 that

relations between Christians and Moslems in Borno State hit an all time low following recent clashes that led to the death of over 20 persons. Moslem fanatics…are opposed to Christian institutions and have vowed to resist a growing trend of evangelical churches in the state, especially Maiduguri.

On December 11, 1998, several hundreds of Muslims attacked three churches, burned some cars and looted shops belonging to Christians. It was in protest against the government decision to allow the teaching of Christian Religious Knowledge (CRK) in public schools, even though Islam is taught as a compulsory subject.

This has been a controversial issue for years in this state. It has even been the subject of litigation between the government and CAN. To avoid further violence, the case was withdrawn. Subsequently, the Muslim governor approved the teaching of CRK, because, as he explained, Nigeria is a secular country. However, not much later he retracted again, for, he said, "It appears some of our respected ulamas [Muslim leaders] have taken the matter out of proportion and have continued to orchestrate their clandestine campaign…."

CAN reported that it had informed the government of the campaign, but no precautions were taken. A spokesman declared, "There is no amount of intimidation, threat, or whatsoever that will stop the

Christians in the state from requesting their constitutional and legitimate right of teaching CRK. We are all prepared to die for a better and truly peaceful tomorrow." We are told further that "The Association of Catholic Media Practitioners appealed to Christians to be calm in the face of alleged attacks, but," the report said, "such calls may be ignored as Christian leaders have told their congregations to defend themselves whenever attacked by Muslim youths. A high-powered [Federal] government delegation has been sent to the state...."106

▲ CONCLUDING REMARKS

Not everything has been told, but it is enough. The picture is clear: It is both unbelievably bloody and muddy. I promised to be as objective as possible in my reporting, but warned that objectivity is difficult to achieve and that facts are usually not merely "facts"—not even under calmer conditions. Did you notice the change in tone in the middle of the Zangon Kataf story, or that of Kaduna City? The reasons for the riots, the perpetrators, the victims, the arrested—all of these receive opposite treatments, depending on the orientation of the reporter. This will become clearer still in the next two volumes, where Muslims and Christians present their opinions.

Though Christians often accuse the *NN*, a government-owned newspaper, of strong Muslim bias,107 I found the reporting of Kaduna 2000, for example, more balanced than I had expected. Certainly it is not as openly biased as the Muslim private magazine *Citizen* that I used for the Zangon-Kataf riot. Neither is it as openly biased as the Christian magazine *TC*. Probably the heavy hand of government information management kept the paper within the bounds of political correctness, though I thought to detect that it occasionally chafes under the burden.

As I peruse the Nigerian situation, I can only sadly concur with the unknown writer who referred to riots as "the most dominant feature" of the Nigerian religious situation. Riots are no longer news. Dele Omotunde wrote, "Religious riots have become a routine event in Nigeria. Burning houses, destroying property, maiming and killing innocent people have become a 'normal' way of religious life. The question is no longer 'if' but 'when'."

"Religious violence," he continued, "has now become one of Allah's or God's unwritten commandments that must be obeyed, at least in Nigeria."[108] Even sadder is the prediction by Toyin Falola that "the religious violence will doubtless continue."[109] No wonder Chris Anyanwu referred to religion as the "quicksand of Nigerian journalism"[110]—as well as, I would add, of Nigerian politics and even of genuine piety.

In closing, I wish to remind you that the above sordid description of Christian-Muslim relations in Nigeria has not been written with any malice in my heart. The goal is not to discredit either or both religions or Africa. I am a Christian with high respect for Islam. I would have no pleasure in discrediting either. Neither is my goal to give Nigerians a bad reputation—not after enjoying their hospitality for thirty years.

My major goal is to help steer Christianity and Islam into positive channels for nation building. In this process, the truth must be told without the restraints of oppressive political correctness. Sweeping ugliness under the carpet is not helpful if we desire healing and reconciliation. The ugly facts of this chapter are the platform from which we seek that healing and reconciliation. Without these facts openly confessed, this monograph series will not serve its purpose and Nigeria's religious problems will not be solved.

This chapter shows that the current state of affairs in Nigeria leads to a literal dead end. After analyzing the perspectives of both religions on the current impasse in the next couple of volumes, we will go on to issues like secularism, shari'a, wholism and pluralism. As the TV anchor pleads, don't go away! You are urged to keep checking my Web site for the appearance of subsequent volumes of this series, but please allow both publisher and myself some time.[111]

▲ NOTES ──────────────────────────────────────

[1] "Faith for Ever after—or No More." *Maclean's*, 17 Dec/2001, p. 2. The failure of Wilson-Smith to recognize the important distinction of church-state relations and religion-state relations renders his statement somewhat dubious in value. Religion and law are as much intertwined in the West as they are in Islam, in that many residual Christian concepts underlie Western legal systems. Religion, of course, has to do with beliefs, faith, doctrine and worldview. Viewed in that context, even in these so-called post-Christian days, the secular influence on the evolving Western law system continues to be heavily influenced by considerations of faith, belief, and worldview. This time it is with a secular orientation that is no less religious than the one it seeks to replace. The mix is really unavoidable.

[2] Of course, Indian statistics would be more impressive, but there neither Christians nor Muslims would even think of claiming majority status, since both are overshadowed by the Hindu colossus. Lebanon provides somewhat of a parallel, but the numbers there are minuscule compared to Nigeria.

[3] This is the common designation for the large southern strip of the north. While the far north has traditionally been dominated by Muslims, the Middle Belt was the home mostly of Traditionalists with pockets of Muslim concentrations. The Traditionalists have mostly switched religion, the majority to Christianity.

[4] Three of the many prominent Christians who have warned the country about such a possibility are Prof. I. Audu, late Ambassador J. T. Yusuf and Dr. C. Abashiya, all three from Muslim backgrounds. (*Today's Challenge*, 5/87, pp. 4–5. J.T. Yusuf, 1995, throughout).

[5] As to the colonial question, see my works of 1979 and 1984.

[6] Falola, p. 168.

[7] H.K.W. Kumm, *The Sudan: A Short Compendium of Facts and Figures about the Land of Darkness,* London: Marshall Brothers, 1907, p. 124. L. Kumm in her "Introduction" to H.K.W. Kumm, 1907, pp. 6-8. For additional reference to Kummania, see Boer, 1979, pp. 126-129; 1984, pp. 36-37.

[8] Boer, 1979, pp. 73, 211-212; 1984, p. 62.

[9] Matthew H. Kukah, *Religion, Politics and Power in Northern Nigeria*, Ibadan: Spectrum Books, 1993, p. 154.

[10] Where such switches took place, it becomes almost impossible to stick to the scheme of "Types of Riots" I employ to make sense of it all. Hence some riots end up under the wrong heading, where the original riot fit properly.

[11] For a fuller review of Maitatsine riots see Falola, pp. 137ff, and Charles Ndiomu (Director), *Religious Disturbances in Nigeria,* Kuru: The National Institute for Policy and Strategic Studies, 1986.

[12] *Tell*, 28 Oct/91, p. 3. *African Concord*, 28 Oct/91, p. 30.

[13] *Newswatch*, 6 May/91, p. 16. Ndiomu, pp. 5, 22-23.

[14] Falola, p. 156. Ndiomu, pp. 18-19.

[15] The MSS has been described as the youth wing of JNI. The late Abubukar Gumi was at one time its "inspirer and guide," according to Mohammed Dahiru Sulaiman, p. 5.

[16] *TC*, Mar-Apr/83, pp. 16-19. Kukah, 1993, pp. 158-159.

[17] J.H. Dandaura, Letter to the Secretary of the Committee Appointed to Investigate the Religious Disturbance of 30th October, 1982, 3 Dec/82.

[18] Christian Association of Nigeria, Kano State Branch. 22 Dec/82, pp. 32-33.

[19] Dare Babarinsa, "Allahu Akbar!" *Tell*, 28 Oct/91, pp. 12-16.

[20] For other reports on this riot see Falola, pp. 211-212, and Karl Maier, *This House Has Fallen: Midnight in Nigeria,* New York: Public Affairs, 2000, pp. 160-165.

[21] *Ibid.*, p. 165.

[22] Marshall, 1997, p. 63. Marshall's book is all about persecution of Christians in the international contemporary society. It is a pity that, in his otherwise splendid book, he devoted only one single page to the Nigerian drama. The Nigerian story appears so little known in the outside world that even a researcher like Marshall apparently failed to realize the enormity of the situation. He later went to Nigeria to see the situation first-hand.

[23] Obed. B. Minchakpu, "Ghosts Haunt Kano." *TC*. No. 3/95, p. 16;

James B. Kantiok, *Muslims and Christians in Northern Nigeria: Political and Cultural Implications for Evangelism,* Unpublished dissertation manuscript for Fuller Theological Seminary, 1999, p. 236; K. Maier, p. 169.

[24] Samuel Uche, "Is Islam Lawlessness?" An interview. *TC,* 3/96, p. 22.

[25] Both contemptuous terms Hausa Muslims sometimes apply to non-Muslims.

[26] For a first-hand report, see Gedege (*initials unknown*), "Kano Needs Divine Intervention," an interview. *TC,* 3/95, p. 23.

[27] Audu Dirambi, "Government Must Wake Up to Her Responsibilities," an interview, *TC,* 3/95, p. 25. See here also for another first-hand report.

[28] For the speech by Governor Muhammed Wase establishing the panel and its terms of reference as well as his interpretation of the event, see M. Wase, *TC,* 3/95, p. 19.

[29] For an example of how the Kano government handles compensation to victims, see interview with Samuel Uche, Chairman of Kano CAN chapter, in which he accuses the government of paying compensation only to those who have "godfathers" and then behind closed doors. He also denies the government's claim to have compensated the family of Akaluka. *TC,* 3/96, p. 22.

[30] Minchakpu, *TC,* 3/96, pp. 16-18.

[31] Uche, p. 26.

[32] CAN, 1987, Appendix E.

[33] The story about this Indian student will be told in more detail in Volume 3.

[34] Jacob Tsado and Yusufu Ari, "Special Investigation: Who Is Trying to Destabilise Islam?" *TC,* 4/87, pp. 16-20, 32.

[35] Maier, K., p. 208.

[36] CAN, Jema'a Local Government Branch, 12 Mar/87. "Jema'a" is the name of the local government area of which Kafanchan is the headquarters.

[37] CAN, Jema'a Branch report. See also Kukah, 1993, Chapter 6 and Falola, pp. 179-182.

[38] CAN Release, 1987, pp. 3-6.

[39] Falola, pp. 182-185.

[40] It should be understood that Hausa traders are almost without exception Muslims.

[41] M. Haruna, 15 Jun/2000, p. 4.

[42] As unlikely as this may seem to outsiders, such demands by police are common in Nigeria. I have faced them several times.

[43] 3/92, pp. 7-8. The incident is typical of northern Muslim insensitivity towards others. How could an experienced man like an emir become so blatantly one-sided, if not for such insensitivity characteristic of northern Muslims? It was an outrageous failure of equanimity.

[44] The quote is not from the letter but from the report in *TC* from which this story is drawn (*TC*, 3/92, pp. 4ff). The definite article is significant: *the jihad*. Nigerian Christians are convinced that a *jihad* is being planned to take over the country. It is only a matter of when it will start. Others would argue that it started long ago.

[45] *TC*, 3/92, pp.4-5.

[46] *TC*, 3/92, p. 10.

[47] *TC*, 3/92, pp. 4-5.

[48] *TC*, 3/92, p. 15.

[49] *TC*, 3/92, pp. 12-13. Muslims protecting Christians against Muslim attackers is a regular feature of these riots. The reverse is true as often.

[50] *TC, 3/92, pp. 13-14.*

[51] *Citizen,* 15 Jun/92.

[52] *Citizen,* 15 Jun/2000, p. 4.

[53] President Obasanjo in a national broadcast. See *NN*, 2 Mar/01, p. 3.

[54] 6 Mar/2000.

[55] *NN*, 10 Jan/2000, p. 14. This almost certainly inflated figure is kind of surprising. The larger Kaduna demonstration in February was allegedly joined by 50,000. One might rather expect a deflated figure in *NN*, given its Muslim orientation. For a follow-up story see *NN*, 14 Jan/2000.

[56] Igiebor, 6 Mar/2000.

[57] The reason for this alleged unbalanced membership is itself a matter of dispute. Gideon Gwani, the Christian Deputy Speaker of the House, claimed it was simply an oversight that needed to be corrected (*NN*, 12 Feb/2000, p. 3). Down below we will hear another explanation by the Muslim Chairman of the committee.

[58] 6 Mar/2000, p. 20.

[59] Awowede, 6 Mar/2000, p. 15

[60] Awowede, 6 Mar/2000, pp. 15-16.

[61] If this sounds incredible or exaggerated, first-hand confessions of similar terrorists in Volume 2 will corroborate that such people do not only exist but are not that rare in the Muslim community, sometimes sponsored by respectable and leading mainstream Muslim organizations.

[62] B.E.E. Debki's report to the EYN, pp. 22-23.

[63] Minchakpu, *CC*, 7 Aug/2000, p. 5.

[64] Emmanuel S. Rabo, "Remembering Sharia Widows," *TC*, 1/2001, pp. 26-27.

[65] Although national magazines like *Newswatch* and *Tell* do not overtly parade themselves as Christian, in the Christian-Muslim struggle they definitely tend to take a pro-Christian position.

[66] *NN*, 31 Jan/2000, p. 1.

[67] *NN*, 5 Feb/2000, p. 9; 20 Feb/2000, p. 24.

[68] *NN*, 19 Feb/2000, p. 10.

[69] *NN*, 20 Feb/2000, p. 24.

[70] *NN*, 23 Feb/2000, pp. 1-2.

[71] *NN*, 26 Feb/2000, pp. 4-5.

[72] *NN*, 29 Feb/2000.

[73] *NN*, 24, 26, 27 Feb/2000. I include various names in these stories for the benefit of those familiar with the culture of names in Nigeria. Names often provide clues as to ethnic origin and religion. Matching names of reporters and other speakers with their reports or comments can provide interesting insights.

74 Debki, pp. 42-74.

75 Dotun Oladipo, "Obasanjo's Tough Stance on Sharia." *Newswatch*, 13 Mar/2000, pp. 20–28.

76 Tunde Asaju, "Counting Their Losses." *Newswatch*, 27 Mar/2000, pp. 28-30., 27.

77 *NN*, 25 Feb/2000, pp. 1-2; 27 Feb/2000, p. 2; 28 Feb/2000, pp. 1-2.

78 Oladipo, 13 Mar/2000.

79 Obasanjo, Broadcast to the nation, 1 Mar/2000.

80 Yahaya and his followers deny his leadership of this sect or even its existence in Nigeria, since Islam supposedly knows of no sectionalism. These are described by his aides as mere journalistic inventions (*TSM*, 27 Sep/92, p. 19). Yahaya himself rejects any recognition of Muslim divisions as a Jewish ploy to create divisions in Islam (Ojudu, p. 36). See also Falola, p. 195.

81 Please be aware that in these volumes there are two Christian Governors who play significant roles. There is this John Madaki, Governor of Katsina, and then there is Yohanna Madaki, one-time Governor of Gongola and Benue states, who subsequently served the Sayawa as their lawyer, while he also plays a role in the aftermath of the Zangon-Kataf episode.

82 Though the Muslim view of Christ differs from the Christian view, they do hold Christ in high esteem as an important prophet. Muslims often seem more jealous of the name of Jesus than do Christians. Perceived insults to Him have more than once provoked Muslims to public demonstrations, even in Great Britain.

83 *Newswatch*, 29 Apr/91, p. 16. *TSM*, 27 Sep/92, p. 15. M. D. Sulaiman, p. 10.

84 Ojudu, p. 36.

85 Ndiomu, pp. 23-26. See also Falola, pp. 153-156, 204, 208; Kukah, 1993, p. 189. See also the section on Tafawa Balewa below, especially the Madaki materials.

86 Falola, pp. 197. Ojudu, p. 36.

[87] Falola, pp. 202-203.

[88] Newswatch, 6 May/91, pp. 10-17. *TC*, no. 1/91, p. 7. Falola, p. 204.

[89] "Death and Destruction," *Newswatch*, 6 May/93, pp. 12, 14.

[90] Falola, pp. 208-209.

[91] *NS*, 20 Apr/94.

[92] *TC*, No. 1/96, p. 7.

[93] *TC*, No. 1/96, pp. 9-12.

[94] Minchakpu, No. 1/96, p. 7.

[95] Minchakpu, 29 Oct/2001.

[96] *TC*, 1/95, pp. 10-11.

[97] *TC*, 1/95, pp. 13-14.

[98] *Nigeria Standard*, 20 Apr/94. My own 20-year interaction with Jos society.

[99] Abdulsalami, 9 Sep/2001.

[100] S. Audu, Vol. 3, No. 2, pp. 1-2.

[101] His need for protection is not necessarily from Muslims but from Christians who may resent his report on Christian violence. It is not his life that may need protection so much as his reputation.

[102] A friend's email report, 9 Sep/2001.

[103] Private email of 10 Sep/2001.

[104] Achi and Peter-Omali, 3 May/2002.

[105] Minchakpu, 26 Aug/2002. Wase, it should be realized, was the site of the original Nigeria-based centre for the Sudan United Mission in 1904. However, Lugard, the first colonial governor of Northern Nigeria, forced the mission to vacate the place due to the danger of Muslim unrest (Boer, 1979, pp. 115, 138-139, 143, 157, 195-197). At that time, Islam wielded the power there. Today, less than a century later, according to Minchakpu, Christians constitute 66% of the population.

[106] *Nigerian News du Jour*, 22 Dec/98. *MM*, Mar/99, pp. 20-21.

[107] See e.g. Wudiri.

[108] *Tell*, 28 Oct/91.

[109] Falola, p. xvii.

[110] *The Sunday Magazine*, 27 Sep/92, p. 4.

[111] www.SocialTheology.com

APPENDICES[1]

THE VIOLENT POLITICS OF RELIGION
AND THE SURVIVAL OF NIGERIA[2]

Press Statement by Ahmadu Bello University Lecturers, 1987

Since last Friday, 6th March, 1987, violent attacks have been launched against life, property and places of worship in most of the major cities and towns of Kaduna State. Churches and mosques; hotels and cinemas; businesses and vehicles; private homes and persons have been attacked, smashed up and systematically set on fire, in an unprecedented campaign of violent religious politics clearly aimed against the survival of our country.

In these seven days many people have been killed and wounded. Many more have been harassed, molested, completely frightened and made totally insecure. Over a hundred churches and a few mosques have been burnt down completely. Right now in Zaria, almost all economic, educational and other activities have stopped. Hundreds of people are on the roads and motor parks and railway stations looking for transport to travel back to their home-towns for safety and security. The basis of normal life has been severely shaken. In spite of reports and warnings from concerned individuals and organizations, three days after the start of the vio-lence, police and security forces were completely absent from the scene. Citizens were left completely at the mercy of the violent mobs. This apparent abdication of responsibility by Government must be taken very seriously.

This type of violent campaign of Muslims against Christians is unprecedented in the history of our country. It directly threatens her continued survival as a single entity.

We, the undersigned citizens of…Nigeria, who have no other country…but this one, have witnessed and personally experienced this violent attack against one of the foundations on which our country exists, namely the *secular nature of the Nigerian State* and its duty to protect the rights of everyone to practice his/her own religion without any hindrance….

In January, 1986, some of us were forced to issue a signed statement warning over the handling of Nigeria's relations with the Organization of Islamic Conference, and the way Israel and the Vatican were being used by sinister and reactionary forces to under-mine the unity of our people and the sovereignty and integrity of our nation. That statement is entitled "*Nigerian Foreign Policy Should Actively Foster Nigerian Unity Based on Our African Identity and Destiny.*" It was pointed out that this campaign of systematic manipulation of religious sentiments is being conducted for the sinister and reactionary purpose of diverting the attention of the people of this country from the urgent tasks of economic recon-struction and the working out of…[*Next few words illegible.*]

In the long term, the purpose of this campaign of political manipulation of religious sentiments is to entrench religious conflicts in all facets of our national life, so that the Nigerian agents of imperialism, working under the cover of Christianity and Islam, financed by Zionism and Arab reaction, can always hold the unity of this country to ransom, build up the forces for its destruction, and ultimately break it up so as to give a serious blow to the movements for democracy, social and national liberation, which are now making great advances all over Africa. The individuals, groups and organizations waging this campaign against the unity of the people of this country, are particularly afraid of, and very hostile to popular mobilization and debate at the grassroots level over who, and what is responsible for what has gone wrong with this country in the last 25 years, and how these retrograde and backward forces and elements can be overcome for genuine economic, social and political progress. They therefore wear the cloak of religion in order to confuse and divert the attention of our people from their harsh conditions of existence, and how to positively transform these conditions in a permanent and systematic fashion.

Our experience of the current events and all evidence available to us, have convinced us that the violence and arson of the last seven days was not the brain work of hooligans. It is…believed to be the latest stage of a campaign which started about ten years ago in the so-called "Shari'a Debate"[3]…in 1976/77.

At that time it was aimed at creating political constituencies for political leadership, whose records showed that they had nothing to offer our people. This strategy failed and therefore they now turn again to the manipulation of religious sentiments and religious symbolism to cover up their complete bankruptcy and failures.

Right now we can see behind the killing, maiming and arson a return to the 1976/77 scenario. Only this time the level of violence and the threat to national security and survival is much higher. But just as 1976/77 was only two to three years away from a return to civilian democracy, so 1986/87 is also only two to three years away from a return to civilian democracy in 1990. The basic difference, however, is that progressive development among the people of Nigeria and the rest of Africa over the last ten years have made these backward and reactionary forces more determined to entrench religious conflict in Nigeria…and to ultimately wreck it….

…This campaign has reached this totally unacceptable and very dangerous level because successive Federal Governments have toyed with one of the foundations on which Nigerian unity exists, namely the secular nature of the Nigerian State and its sacred… [*not legible*]. A strong impression has been created that some organizations and individuals can, with arrogance and impunity, incite and threaten people of other religious beliefs and will get away with, at most, only verbal reprimands or appeals to be tolerant.

…This campaign of violent religious politics has reached the very dangerous levels it has because several powerful media organs, particularly the Federal Radio Corporation of Nigeria, Kaduna, have been allowed to be used by a tiny backward oligarchy which survives on inciting one section of Nigeria against another. Anybody who listens…since January 1986 and particularly since Monday, March 9, 1987, knows that something sinister and violent was being systematically planned against the unity of…Nigeria and against the peace and stability of the country.

We, the undersigned, therefore want to warn, in a very solemn way, all our brothers and sisters…that we are fast coming to the brink of catastrophe. The events of the last seven days are very serious and very dangerous for our individual and collective survival. All those citizens committed to the unity of this country, for which so much blood has been shed, have to stand up and make a choice between fear, timidity and inertia in the face of systematic destruction of the foundation of our nation, and a determined struggle to crush these forces of destruction and save our country and our future.

We call on the Federal Military Government (FMG) to shed all ambiguities and hesitation, and to declare and reaffirm that the

Nigerian State is SECULAR and one of its most fundamental responsibilities is to *protect the right of every citizen and resident to practice the religion of their choice.* We call on the FMG to implement this decisively and clearly in practice by identifying publicly, and punishing according to the law all the rich and powerful individuals who are known to be behind this campaign of violent religious politics aimed at destroying our country.

We call on the FMG to ensure, in all parts of the country, the security of life and property and places and of freedom of belief and worship of everyone.

We call on the FMG to affirm and promote the exercise of the fundamental human rights of individuals and the collective self-defense of all the people against any form of aggression, be it external or internal.

We call on the FMG to make, as a matter of utmost urgency, full reparations to all those who have suffered damages. In particular, we ask...[*not legible*] that the right of facilities for worship by all religious groups is restored and guaranteed in all places where they have been destroyed.

We are convinced that the sinister and utterly reactionary forces behind this campaign of violent religious politics with the aim of destroying our country are made up of a tiny oligarchy determined to maintain its power, wealth and privileges at all costs, including violent and well-organized mobs in the name of religion. We are also convinced that the majority of the people of this country and the popular organizations are capable of being mobilized to overcome them and defend the unity of our people and the integrity of our country. We therefore call upon the Nigerian Labour Congress to mobilize all the workers of this country around a campaign against religious and all sectional politics.

LONG LIVE THE FEDERAL REPUBLIC OF NIGERIA.[4]

▲ APPENDIX 2

SUBMISSION TO THE KADUNA STATE COMMISSION OF
ENQUIRY INTO THE RECENT DISTURBANCES IN KADUNA
STATE[5]

Chief Daniel Gowon, 1987

Waves of Vandalistic Campaigns

There were *FOUR* waves in all. The first wave of the campaign
of terror comprised of multiple of hundreds of *"Jihad / Allahu
Akbar"*-chanting individuals whose job from what they did was
pulling down the fence, destruction and setting the old Church and
first Hausa church to be put up in the North, which was built in
1929, ablaze and some private homes. Every moveable item in the
Church was taken out of the Church and burnt. Initially they
thought the carpet in the Church donated by Brigadier S.
Ogbemudia on behalf of Bendel State Government in 1973, would
easily catch fire. Despite dousing with petrol, it burnt little, but the
Church became full of soot. All windows and doors were deformed,
burnt or smashed and crosses stolen or broken. An attempt to collapse the Church proved abortive. Other waves (3) performed similar acts of banditry and vandalism. In all, about 21 homes were burnt
in Wusasa. Most of the Christian selected occupants of Wusasa…
were chased out and ejected from their homes by the vandals.

How the Family House[6] Was Set Ablaze

The vandals forced the gate…they started their business by
breaking all the glasses to the doors and windows and that gave
them the opportunity of pouring petrol on all the curtains and setting the house on fire…. Most of those…are boys under the age of
15 years with their guides…. They used all sorts of dangerous

weapons such as daggers, cutlasses, broken bottles, stones, sticks, etc. I was wounded while trying to escape....

My glory and joy was that there was no loss of life recorded within the community. All the family excluding myself escaped unhurt with our two vehicles, but was unable to remove anything from the house including all the souvenirs belonging to one time Head of State.... All in all the losses sustained materialistic was colossal.

Molestation and Provocation of People

Almost every one in Wusasa was molested, especially the Christians. They were asked to recite the Muslim creed. Some were beaten...and left for dead, naked on the street. Mrs. Denejo Ibrahim and Mrs. Asaber Naandeti were victims, while some were ruffled and cut.

Molestation and provocation were definite indications towards a total collapse of law and order. These were what fueled and heightened the one-sided sectarian conflict inflicted on Wusasa. I thank God that my people turned the other cheek. Had their reaction been any different, only God knows where it would have led.

I want this honourable body to note that although Christians were the target, some Muslims suffered just as much, for example Alhaji Aiyelero and Deputy Commissioner of Police, Alhaji Isa Inusa had their property burnt. Justice Bello was ruffled and several others. These events occurred within the area of my jurisdiction.

▲ APPENDIX 3 —————————————————————————

DEATH AND DESTRUCTION AT BAPTIST SEMINARY,
KADUNA, IN 2000

Yusuf Gwadah

The students and staff at the Baptist Seminary were aware that there was going to be a march on that Monday by the Christians to oppose the attempts to get shari'a into Kaduna State. However, the authorities of the seminary refused to allow them to participate. Some time about the middle of the day, they started hearing noise coming from the town side of the seminary and learned that there was trouble going on. They could also see smoke billowing up on that side. After a little while, a group of young Muslim boys gathered up outside of the seminary and it appeared that they were going to cause trouble. The school officials called the seminary students together and told them that they were going to try to defend the school. The seminary is totally surrounded by a concrete wall about eight feet tall. However, the officials felt that it was better to keep the Muslims some distance away from even the wall. Therefore, all or nearly all of the students went outside the gate and lined up in front of the seminary to try to defend the school. There were about 150 students in the seminary and all or nearly all participated in the defense. The Muslims lined up not much more than 100 feet away and they started fighting.

The only weapons that either side had were stones and sticks. I think some of the Muslims also had some knives. However, the battle was basically a contest of throwing stones. The Muslims would throw stones at the seminary boys and the seminary boys would throw them back. Every once in a while, a group of the Muslims would make a rush for the seminary and when they came close enough to the seminary boys they would fight with sticks. If one of seminary boys fell down during the fight, the Muslims would all rush toward him and that would require the other seminary boys coming to his defense.

At one point, the seminary boys looked up and saw one of their fellow students coming toward the seminary from town. He had to pass through the Muslim mob or go around them some way. However, the Muslims spotted him, chased him down and started beating him. Although he was out of their zone of safety, the seminary boys rushed out in mass to where they were beating the boy. They drove the Muslims away enough to get the student and take him inside the compound.

Later that day, a Muslim came riding a motor cycle up a certain small road that was apparently under the control of the seminary students. It was obvious that he was a Muslim so the students told him to go back. However, he refused and said that he wanted to go join the fighters. When he tried to pass through, he was attacked and beaten and apparently killed. I witnessed that incident. I had never seen anyone die like that and it was very unsettling. I should also point out here that all of the defenders of the seminary were not seminary students. Other "Christians" in the area who knew the battle was going on came to the seminary to try to defend it. In fact, many people came to the seminary for safety because they thought it would be well defended.

The fighting of the seminary students was primarily defensive. They were simply trying to defend the seminary. However, there were others who became much more aggressive as illustrated by the killing of the boy on the motorcycle.

A couple of other things were going on during the battle. The telephones were still working in the seminary. The principal was able to get through to the local police chief and told him that they were under attack. However, the police chief who was a Muslim said that there was trouble everywhere and there was not much he could do. The principal talked to the Baptist Mission headquarters in

Ibadan and explained their desperate condition. He eventually was able to reach Professor Abaje, who is the president of the Baptist Seminary in Ogbomoso and also the personal chaplain of President Obasanjo. Prof. Abaje was able to reach President Obasanjo and the president called the police chief in Kaduna. The police chief told him that there had been some trouble but everything was under control. There has been a whole lot of discussion about this Muslim police chief's handling of this crisis. Many Christians are convinced he knew about the plans for this in advance. It is generally thought at the very least that he did not handle this thing very evenly.

The second thing that happened that day was that the Muslim village chief of that area kept shuttling back and forth between the seminary boys and the attacking Muslim boys. He would come over to the Christian side and say,

"Please don't fight. We are all one people. We should not be fighting one another." The seminary boys would tell him,

"Sir, we don't want to fight. They are the ones who are attacking us. If they will go away, we will stop fighting. We have no desire to fight anyone." The chief would then walk over to the other side and talk to them. He apparently shuttled back and forth several times that day. He reported to the seminary boys that the Muslims were very stubborn and were refusing to listen to him.

This battle went on for two or three hours. It was a strange atmosphere. It was not really a very angry mob. It was almost like a game. One group would be on the offense and the other was on the defense. One group would get the upper hand for a while and then the other group would get the upper hand. The two groups were fairly evenly matched and just played their deadly game for several hours. However, eventually the mob grew weary of the game and left. When they did, some of the students were able to take the seriously wounded student whom they had rescued to the Air Force hospital that was about a mile or so away from the seminary compound. Shortly after he got there, the student died. He was a first-year seminary student. So there was at least one casualty on both sides that first day. Things were relatively calm at the seminary on Monday evening. They all tried to rest but it was difficult to sleep.

The next morning about 6:30 or so, the Muslims attacked again. This time they brought a much bigger mob. There were hundreds of Muslims. The seminary boys once again went outside the wall to try to defend the seminary. During this battle, there was a thick smoke that was hanging over the area. It was so thick at times that it partially obscured the enemies only a hundred feet or so away. Though they fought valiantly, they were greatly outnumbered on Tuesday. They kept being driven back against the wall. They would fight and drive the Muslims back a little less each time. Finally around 11:30 AM, they realized that they could no longer defend the seminary from outside the fence. Therefore, they all withdrew inside the compound wall and shut the big metal door.

All during this time I did not know what was happening to my wife and two children. Someone had put a tall ladder up against the compound wall in the back. The wall must be at least eight feet high. And while the battle had been getting heavy outside the wall, the school officials had decided to evacuate the wives and children and others over that back fence. So by the time the students had to retreat inside the wall, nearly everyone else had escaped over the back wall. The area behind the seminary was more of a bush area. The few houses in the area were primarily owned by Christians. There was an Air Force base about a mile away on that side of the seminary so the seminary families, including one American Baptist missionary family, trekked to that base.

Once the Muslims got access to the wall, they did two things. First, they brought in some kind of heavy device and started pounding away at the wall. They eventually broke a hole in the wall. However, apparently the hole was a bit small at first and they were afraid to pour through the hole at first, because they knew that the seminary boys were on the other side of the wall waiting for them. No one wanted to be the first person through the fence.

The second thing they did was to throw petrol over the wall onto one of the dormitory buildings which was very close to the wall. As soon as they were able to soak the thing down with petrol, they somehow managed to throw some burning object over the fence that caught that dormitory building on fire. So during the latter part of the battle, one of the seminary buildings was burning inside the compound.

By this time, it was obvious that the students would not be able to save the seminary. Therefore they started withdrawing and going over the back fence a few at a time. However, some had to stay near the breach in the fence to keep up the noise and keep throwing stones in order to discourage the Muslims from coming inside the fence until most of the students had escaped over the wall. I was one of the last ones to leave the front lines, but there was still one or two there when he ran for the back fence and went over. Apparently all of the students who were inside the compound were able to safely escape over the wall.

Since there was a lot of smoke and noise, it took a while for the Muslims to actually come inside the compound. However, they eventually came inside and started burning buildings. Apparently at first, they were just burning buildings. However, when they discovered that there were no people inside the buildings, they started looting the dormitories and houses before burning them. Later when the students were able to go through the burnt rubble, it was obvious that the Muslims had carried away anything that they considered to be valuable.

It took a little while for the students to get to the Air Force base. The soldiers stationed there had all been waiting on orders from above to move into the town and try to stop some of the looting and killing. However, they never did receive any orders. Finally after the seminary boys came straggling in, some of the officers decided that they would do something on their own. So they took a vehicle and some troops and drove to the seminary. When they got there, they caught many of the Muslims inside and were able to arrest about twenty of them. Some of them were brought back to the Air Force base where I saw some of them. They had apparently been beaten by the soldiers very seriously. They were later turned over to the police but no one knows what happened to them after that.

When the Air Force soldiers got to the seminary, the Muslims had destroyed everything except three missionary residences that were on the back part of the compound near the ladder where the people had escaped. Apparently they were systematically going through the compound looting and burning. Fortunately, the soldiers got there before they got to that part of the compound. However, they burned everything else. All the dormitories were destroyed and everything in them which had not been looted. The administration building and the library and all ten thousand books in it were destroyed. There was absolutely nothing left of the seminary.

The next day, when I and some other students got back to the seminary, we found the bodies of two more of our fellow students. These students had apparently been in an annex which was a short distance away. They had apparently been trying to get to the main campus but were ambushed by the Muslims and killed. A security guard and the sixteen-year-old son of another employee of the seminary were also killed. There were also several of the community people who died in or around the seminary.

▲ APPENDIX 4 ───────────────────────────────

KADUNA'S KILLING FIELDS[7]
Bala Abdullahi and Kayode Kolade, 2000

By Thursday when Kaduna State Government relaxed the curfew from 24 hours to 12, and inaugurated a 5-man judicial commission to investigate this week's two days of rioting by Christian and Muslim youth, hundreds of people lay dead in the streets of Kaduna. Another hundred more were wounded and the city reduced to rubble. Kaduna's latest pogrom, the fourth since 1987, is no doubt the worst in terms of scope of damage and loss of human lives.

President Olusegun Obasanjo had to go on the air Wednesday to strongly condemn the carnage, describing it as barbaric, criminal, unpatriotic and unwarranted display of religious zealotry. The two-day riots climaxed weeks of agitation for and against adoption of Sharia as the legal system of the state. While Muslim-dominated local governments strongly supported sharia adoption, those from the Southern part which are predominantly Christian strongly opposed it.

By the time the State House of Assembly committee on Sharia concluded public sitting last Thursday, Christians apparently believed that the state government had taken a stand on Sharia. It was based on this assumption that the leadership of Christian Association of Nigeria (CAN), Kaduna State chapter, last Sunday February 20, passed a message to churches in the town calling Christians to meetings at various points.

The meetings took place at St. John's Cathedral, Unguwar Rimi, St. Joseph Cathedral and Catholic Social Centre both in the heart of Kaduna metropolis as well as Catholic Resource Centre, Abakwa. As early as 6:30 that Monday morning, Christian youth, men and women assembled at the designated points to receive the last word from their leaders as to what to do.

At the end of the sermon, they went chanting "Rest in peace Sharia." Many of them also carried placards with inscriptions opposing the call by Muslim leaders to adopt Sharia. Throngs of demonstrators filed up Independence Way, Ibrahim Taiwo Road and Ahmadu Bello Way. Another headed down College Road apparently towards Sir Kashim Ibrahim House, the official residence of the state governor.

The protestors forced their way in by scaling its walls and overpowering the handful of security men on duty. There they demanded an assurance from deputy Governor Stephen Shekari that Kaduna would not take a cue from Zamfara State which adopted Sharia as its legal system last year.

Mr. Shekari appealed to them to be calm and to show understanding as the state government had not taken a decision on the Sharia issue. He advised them to direct whatever their grievance was to the consultative committee on Sharia set up by the state government. The committee, he said, comprised both Christian and Muslim clerics.

Views vary as to which group started the molestation and subsequent vandalization and killings. Mr. Sa'idu Dogo, Secretary of the Kaduna State branch of the Christian Association of Nigeria (CAN) claimed that Christians were attacked near the central market by militant Muslim youth. "Initially we (Christians) retreated, but when the attack continued and property was set ablaze, we had no choice but to retaliate almost spontaneously," he said.

But Dr. Sirajo Abdulkarim, member of the Islamic Trust of Nigeria, disagreed, saying that aside from the graphic misunderstanding and misconception on the part of the Christians on what Sharia is all about, "they attacked us (Muslims) as they exercised their fundamental human right to protest against Sharia along the way."

In his own account, the acting Secretary-General of Jama'atul Nasril Islam (JNI), Malam Ja'afaru Makarfi while speaking with newsmen said that "until the burning of a mosque along Ibrahim Taiwo Road the Christian anti-Sharia protests, were all peaceful. This singular act provoked the Muslims to revenge."

Invariably, the claims and counter-claims turned into a confrontation, with men, women, and children running helter-skelter searching for safe havens. Like a bush fire, the religious skirmishes spread to all nooks and crannies of the city, leaving scores dead, and hundreds of thousands wounded or maimed, while property including churches and mosques worth millions of Naira were destroyed.

Notwithstanding the spirited efforts of the state government to restore order, the self-styled "liberal state" was blasted into world news headlines. A dusk to dawn curfew was announced but hostilities continued.

The senseless human waste spread through Monday night and all of Tuesday as more mobile Police and army units poured into troubled neighbourhoods to restore peace and inject sanity. The state government in another desperate effort to save lives and property issued another press release with...the Deputy Governor, Stephen R. Shekari appealing for calm and understanding while the curfew was extended from 12 noon to 6 am the next day.

The deputy governor stated *inter alia*:

> *following an assessment which I undertook this morning (Tuesday) to some parts of Kaduna metropolis and environs, it has become absolutely necessary for me to again caution the people of this state. It is disheartening to observe that in spite of the passionate appeals made to citizens on the need to eschew violence of any form, there are strong indications that the senseless destruction of lives and property will not ordinarily abate.*

In view of this, he said, "I have accordingly directed the closure of all offices and businesses forthwith. No movement would be allowed into and within the metropolis with effect from 12:00 noon." He warned that anybody who flouted those orders would have himself to blame. "People should remain in their residences until further notice," the statement concluded.

Despite the curfew and passionate appeals from eminent religious leaders, looting and killings continued at Tudun Wada, Rigasa, Unguwar Sanusi and Sabo, Unguwar Sarki, Kawo areas of the state capital where streets were littered with human corpses, and churches and mosques torched, shops and stalls were razed to ashes, while vehicles were terribly vandalized.

Rev. (Dr.) Matthew Hassan Kukah, National Secretary General of the Catholic Secretariat of Nigeria expressed utmost sadness over the incident but he said he saw it coming but put the blame on the doorsteps of some governors who were playing politics with Sharia. The violence of the week was "a signal to the political class that this fire could consume everything," he said, adding that though Sharia was a legitimate demand by Muslims, they must follow the constitutional process in prosecuting it.

He claimed like other Christians that the legitimate Christian demonstration that went out of control, was engineered by hoodlums, and expressed optimism that Nigeria has an incredible capacity to recover from the bestiality as Muslims and Christian leaders are signing peace pacts which enjoin followers of the two religions to live together in peace.

Similarly, the Sultan of Sokoto and President-General, Supreme Council for Islamic Affairs, Alhaji Muhammadu Maccido and Emir of Zazzau, Alhaji Shehu Idris in separate addresses called on both Muslims and Christians to exercise restraint and live in peace with one another. Both traditional rulers stressed that "what we fail to achieve through peace, there is no way it could be achieved through violence." Both religions preach peace and tolerance of one another.

This is Kaduna. The story of a self-styled liberal state where murderous adventure, wanton destruction of lives and property had in the last few days halted business and commercial activities. The story of Kaduna is that of frustration, humiliation and uncertainties. It is a story of man's inhumanity to man in the name of religion. This was how a journalist from the Lagos-Ibadan press axis summed up the tragic drama in Kaduna, a strategic city in the heart of Northern Nigeria.

Mr. Ismalia Bitrus, narrating his ordeal to the *New Nigerian Weekly* lamented over the whereabouts of his two children who are yet to return from school since Monday when the riot started.

But to Sunday Jonah, it was a horrendous crime as he painfully gave details of how his elder brother Gregg Jonah set out on that fateful early Monday morning for the office and bidding the family farewell and pleading with his 3-month pregnant wife to take the children to school on time, but never returned home.

But that of Ismaila Badru was more graphic as the wife in tears narrated how her husband and breadwinner "was butchered in cold blood in my presence and painfully watched by our two daughters aged 4-6 years."

At the 44 Nigerian Army reference Hospital, where many people took refuge, their stories were agonizingly reflected in their narration. Many claimed to have seen humiliation, borne misery and had been mentally tortured for days.

The sense of frustration was evident in Emeka Amadi's narration of how he and his apprentices watched helplessly from a hideout away from his electronics shop as hoodlums broke in, looted some electronics and set the shop ablaze. He stressed that "as soon as peace returned, I am leaving Kaduna and the North generally, let them continue with their Sharia."

An account was also given of an unidentified man at Tudun Wada on Tuesday who went to his two children's school to take them home. On his way he fell into the hands of the rioters. He was ordered to give up the two children and was himself macheted to death in the presence of his children who thereafter were released to go home.

The story of Malam Dauda Adamu Kiru who narrowly escaped death was equally graphic. He told the *New Nigerian* that he came to Kaduna specifically to trade in the weekly Monday market, Kakuri. He said at about 3 p.m Monday, when news reached him that Christians were protesting the purported adoption of Sharia in Kaduna Sate, he and five others from Kiru in Kano state sensed trouble, adding that as they were contemplating what to do, there was a sudden stampede in the market.

He said they resolved to trek to the residence of a relation at Nasarawa in Chukun Local Government where they hoped to take refuge until the situation improved. But unknown to them, Nasarawa is predominantly inhabited by Christians with a handful of Muslims scattered here and there. They hardly slept that Monday night and on Tuesday as early as 6 a.m. the battle line had been drawn. The Muslims gathered at one end of the suburb while the Christians whose population was four times bigger took up position at the other end. While the cat and mouse game lasted, three representatives from the Christian side came on to them for a peaceful talk and succeeded in convincing them that they had lived together for over 30 years as brothers and sisters and there was no cause for them now to see each other as enemies. They all agreed but, unknown to them, the resolution was a ploy to gain time for reinforcement to arrive from adjoining villages.

He said, 15 minutes after the agreement, the whole area was besieged by youths carrying weapons including sophisticated guns. "They began to shoot indiscriminately and before we knew it, they overpowered us, there was nowhere to run to because we were surrounded," said Malam Dauda.

He added that in the ensuing commotion, he along with his host and one other person he did not know scaled the wall of a neighbour who was an Igbo man. It was the Igbo man who provided them cover in his bedroom until Wednesday afternoon when the military intervened. Dauda said Allah having saved him he would never return to Kaduna. His story could easily have been told also by Christians who lived in areas dominated by Muslims.

At about 2 p.m., Tuesday, Muslim youth stormed the Ibukun Oluwa Baptist church in Abakpa, burning it and the living quarters in the premises. Eye witnesses told the *New Nigerian Weekly* that a driver with the National Electric Power Authority (NEPA) had his throat sliced and burnt for daring to challenge the youth.

Their action, according to residents was to revenge the attack on Muslims elsewhere in the metropolis. They did not stop at the church but headed for nearby Gondola hotel and all residential houses believed to be inhabited by Christians on Jaji road they also torched.

This spontaneous reaction on Monday unconsciously had set the tone of events to come the next day. Apprehensive of what would come, most people in the area, women and children had begun to evacuate to the Nigeria Defence Academy where security was guaranteed. The men remained behind to watch over property.

Reports reaching U/Shanu had it that Christians from Abakpa had taken up arms and by 11 a.m. had reached Dan Kano road in U/Shanu. The incident on Dan Kano road was an ugly one. The Muslim youth made sure they destroyed every house they believed was inhabited by Christians. They destroyed a small church on Dan Kano road, a beer parlour in the adjoining street, the car of the owner of the church who lived together with other Muslims at No. 25 Dan Kano road which they thrice threatened to set on fire but for the pleading of Muslim elders.

After the Tuesday's fracas, alignment afterwards had been by one's religious leaning, until the news of Wednesday night that security agents had together with Christians brought in some boxes which the Muslims suspected were arms. The Muslims reached the Saint Peter's church where the boxes were deposited requesting to see their contents. That was shortly after Christian leaders in Abakpa had sent an emissary to the Hausa leaders seeking a peaceful resolution of the crisis.

Unconfirmed reports as at press time had it that the boxes were opened in the presence of the Muslim youth who apparently were satisfied that they contained no weapons after all. Peace talks were started, and tension was doused in the process, but residents of these two suburbs still were not comfortable following reports of looting in the night of Thursday.

People who took refuge at the 44 Nigerian Army Reference Hospital were still lamenting their losses in human life and property, and lack of food and shelter, when some Nigerien[8] nationals stormed the barrack. The vigilant military authorities arrested three of them, while one was shot dead as he struggled to escape.

…Despite efforts by the Kaduna State government and security agencies and appeals by religious leaders and eminent Nigerians for cessation of hostilities, the crisis spilled over to adjoining cities. *New Nigerian Weekly* learnt that a teacher with Al-HudaHuda College, Zaria, Mr. Musa Bakan was killed following a spillover of the bloody Kaduna religious riot into Zaria. The deceased was attacked and killed at his residence Wednesday at the premises of the college by an irate mob who also burnt his private car.

Confirming the incident, the Assistant Commissioner of Police in-charge of Zaria, Mr. Suleiman Lawal said already the corpse of the victim had been recovered and taken to Ahmadu Bello University Teaching Hospital (ABU), Zaria.

He said about 11 people had so far been wounded including a police inspector who was stabbed at the scene of the disturbances, which spread to Zaria on Tuesday night.

In its concerted efforts to get to the root of this week's mayhem, the Kaduna State government has set up a 5-man judicial commission of inquiry to investigate the immediate and remote causes of the religious unrest. Swearing in members of the commission on Thursday, the deputy governor, Mr. Stephen Shekari said it was unfortunate that people who should know better about what the two main religions stand for which according to him is peace, love for one another and tolerance engaged themselves in senseless killings.

The commission, he said, would advise on how to "put such acts behind us once and for all in order to enable us to forge ahead with our development programmes." The commission which has four weeks to conclude its assignment is under the chairmanship of Justice Ja'afaru Dalhat. Other members are Alhaji Akilu Idris, Mr. P.Y. Lolo, Mr. Victor Gwani and Alhaji Tukur Usman. Mr. Dominic G. Yahaya would serve as secretary, while Mr. Gamaliel Kure is the commission's counsel.

This is the fourth time in two decades that Kaduna's hot pot of religious politics has boiled over. The first was in 1987 in the College of Education, Gidan Waya, Kafanchan where one Reverend Bako while delivering a sermon allegedly made a blasphemous statement against the person and prophecy of Prophet Muhammad (P.B.U.H.). At that moment, the handful of Muslims present including a lady challenged him. A free-for-all fight ensued spreading pretty fast like a wild fire into Kafanchan township and to other local governments like Zaria, Kaduna and Birnin Gwari among others.

The blood trail of the first crisis has been followed by others. In 1992 the Atyeb community of Zangon Kataf local government and the Hausa community who have been living together and intermarried for several decades took up arms against each other. Zangon town was destroyed with more than 1,000 lives lost. Scores of refugees returning to Kaduna and Zaria towns with machete and gun wounds inflamed passion and the spillover nearly consumed the entire city of Kaduna.

The 1987 and 1992 incidents are supposed to serve as a big lesson in the danger of religious bigotry and ethnic cleansing. Alas, another incident took place in the historical town of Kafanchan over the installation of the new emir of Kafanchan, Alhaji Isa Mohammed, who succeeded his late father early in 1999. The people of Jema'a who claimed to be the original indigenes of the area had been agitating for self-determination and a chiefdom of their own independent of the emirate system. The heavy loss of lives and property is still fresh in the minds.

▲ APPENDIX 5 ————————————————

ESCALATION OF RAGE[9]

Onimisi Alao, 2000

Someone who had known Rigasa, a suburb of Kaduna metropolis for a long time and visited the place early afternoon of Thursday February 24 said: "Anyone who sees Rigasa now and still chooses to live there must be joking as no normal human being will want the place after this material and human wreckage."

The observation made on the fourth day of tension in the whole of Kaduna metropolis, following the Monday-Tuesday violent clashes between people opposed to Sharia, an Islamic legal system being canvassed by the Muslim communities.

A visit to the place by the *New Nigerian on Sunday* hours after confirmed that observation. Stench of burnt human bodies that still littered the place was thick enough to push anyone back. Turning towards the ravaged hitherto sprawling Rigasa from the Bakin Ruwa/Nnamdi Azikiwe Expressway end and Abuja Road in Rigasa, half a kilometre away lay nine human corpses. Between Abuja Road and Naira Road were nineteen corpses, most of them by the Rigasa main road and the rest on the outlining streets but visible from the main road.

For about six kilometres, the residential houses which still stood could not possibly outnumber those that have gone up in flames.

Hausa-Fulani Muslims could be seen in the houses that were still habitable, some of them discussing in groups. Some were gathered for the 1 p.m. prayer, but apart from them, virtually all people of other tribes, made up of Kaje, Igbo and Yoruba had left the town either because their houses had been burnt or because they suddenly were too lonely and afraid of what might happen to them if they remained.

Human destruction was less as you come out of Rigasa into its adjoining Asikolaiye, Angwa Sanusi, Tudun Wada and Tudun Nupawa, but losses suffered by individual traders, churches and hotels is enormous. While only few churches and hotels/bars remain unburnt in these places, traders in certain strategic business streets either had their shops burnt down or, if the shops were owned by someone who enjoys the arsonist's sympathy, the contents are drawn out into the streets and burnt.

The popular Chanchangi corner area of the long and winding Ibrahim Taiwo Road is popular for all sizes and models of second hand refrigerators and other household products. The refrigerators in their thousands now lie in a burnt waste.

The first five houses on the left as you get into New Bida Road of Tudun Nupawa from the new fire station end have been burnt down while about half the number of shops on the entire stretch of that road were emptied into the streets and burnt. Curiously, unlike Lagos Street where most of the shop owners had called to see what had become of their shops or could be retrieved from the wreckage, the charred contents of the shops of New Bida Road remain on the road, as at Thursday afternoon, with the few cars using the road having to meander round the wrecked heaps.

On vantage Lagos Street, similar destruction was seen on all sides. If one stood where the road entered Ibrahim Taiwo Road, around the Sheik Abubakar Gumi Central Market, since traders vacated the market following the on-going reconstruction of the market, many of the traders had been using both sides of the two streets for their business activities. The hundreds of fairly permanent shops and thousands of makeshift stalls on the two streets now lie so flat on the ground an observer could mistake the wreckage for a bulldozer destruction, but for the burnt ashes.

On the western side of popular St. Joseph Cathedral Church stood three carcasses of burnt cars. Of course, all the stalls on that side of the road are a burnt ruins while the large Abdulrahman Labaran Electronic store with its stock of new television and radio sets and other electronic gadgets of varying sizes had been similarly destroyed. Most of the other shops down about one and a half kilometres of Lagos Street to Abuja roundabout had their stock brought onto the street and burnt.

The Ibrahim Taiwo Road part of central market known for its sewing machines and materials has also been burnt, with two bloated human bodies still lying around as at Thursday.

Kaduna's prime commercial district, the Ahmadu Bello Way is a scene of destruction of a different dimension. While the makeshift market around Leventis was sore, the only other shops that were safe from Leventis roundabout to Katsina road are those of steel doors and burglar proof too strong for the vandals to open. On this stretch of Ahmadu Bello Way, big names in business have been substantially weakened. Headquarters of Kaduna's long known confectionery outfit, Nanet, lay in ruins. Four cars of a nearby motor sales company were completely burnt with the windscreens of several others within the premises smashed.

More pitiable is another motor sales company close by which has all its cars, numbering not less than sixty, completely burnt. The massive three-story structure on Ibrahim Taiwo Road by Ahmadu Bello Way housing another of Labaran Electronics sales outfit was not spared.

The shops in Ramat Shopping Mall on Kano Road that could be opened had their contents brought out and smashed with a failed attempt actually made at burning some of the shops. Failed attempts were similarly made at burning the St. Joseph Catholic Cathedral. The large Kano Road mosque beside the church would have been in complete ruin save for the fact that the fire put to burn it succeeded in finishing the carpets. The entire length of the street separating the mosque and the church which has for years served as home for "Kano Road beggars" has also been burnt, with the dozens of beggars now taking refuge on the veranda of houses close to the Kano Road bus stop.

Along Abeokuta road in the same Kaduna City centre, three churches laid in burnt waste with the fourth one having its furniture and stationery brought out before they were set on fire.

Down Sardauna Crescent bus stop, some dozen houses have been burnt, including a large two storey office and business complex not more than a few months old. An eyewitness said further loss was prevented by residents who teamed up, irrespective of religious leaning, to ward off the rampaging youth. He disclosed however that two lives were lost to the rampage.

"I can't agree that violence could erupt and spread to almost all the areas of Kaduna in that enormous swoop as we have seen," said someone. "Except those in the GRAs,[10] I have not seen anyone who did not have a taste of trouble that Monday when it all started." He concluded in these words: "Some influential figures are behind this thing. They had a score to settle and this has been their time."

▲ APPENDIX 6 ───────────────────────

AVOIDABLE CARNAGE IN KADUNA[11]

Umar Sanda, 2000

Residents of Kaduna woke up last Monday and began their daily chores oblivious of the crisis ahead. Children had been taken to schools, workers had gone to work and traders had gone to the markets. Many had seen processions heading towards Lugard Hall, the seat of the State Assembly and Sir Kashim Ibrahim House, the offices and official residence of the State Governor.

The procession appeared peaceful. It was not much different from the processions they had almost gotten used to seeing since the State Assembly inaugurated a Special Committee to collate public opinion about the request by some Muslims for the "introduction" of Sharia in the State's legal system. The only difference was that last Monday's processions were much longer, and they headed towards more than one direction. The processions of the previous weeks had been shorter, comprising delegates from one or two local governments at a time, and they headed straight to the State House of Assembly. Their missions were to express their support for the call to introduce the Sharia in Kaduna State.

By last week, when the Committee wound up its public sitting, it appeared that the proponents of *sharia* had carried the day, going by a number of factors. In the first place, when the issue of *sharia* was first discussed at the State Assembly and a decision was taken to constitute an ad-hoc committee, the Christian legislators declined membership of the proposed committee. The assembly was not deterred by the refusal of the Christian members of the Honourable Assembly to participate. It went ahead and constituted an all-Muslim committee. That was the first cause of worry for the Christians about the objectivity of the report that the committee was going to submit.

Secondly, and perhaps resulting from the initial loss of confidence in the impartiality of the committee, the Christians decided to ignore the committee when it started its public sitting. Thus, while Muslim delegations from each of the state's 23 local governments were trooping to Lugard Hall to express support for the *sharia*, a very few Christians bothered to go and express their opposition to the request for the introduction of the *sharia*.

Thus, by the time the committee wound up its sitting, the general impression was that there were more people rooting for *sharia* in the state. When this realization dawned on the Christian leadership, an attempt was made to save the situation. And that attempt was to gather as many Christians as possible to go and make their position on the *sharia* very clear to the government—legislators and the executive.

Apparently, the Christian leadership realized very late in the day that in a democracy, it is those opinions that are publicly articulated and are seen to be shared by the majority of the people that carry the day. They could not expect the State Assembly Committee on *sharia* to come out with a report that would favour them especially that they did not, unlike the Muslims, take it upon themselves to impress it on the Committee that they had a large constituency and that that constituency was opposed to the *sharia*.

The appeal by the Christian leadership in the state to all Christians to congregate at selected churches as early as six in the morning on Monday to go on a peaceful demonstration was one way the leaders thought could remedy their earlier mistake. But barely four hours later, what was planned as a peaceful demonstration had gone violent. Many lives were lost and property worth hundreds of millions of naira destroyed.

Was the demonstration the best means of getting their position across to the government? If the State Assembly appeared to have made up its mind to get *shari'a* introduced, could the same be said of the executive arm of the government? Was the call to demonstrate shrouded in secrecy? Where were the state security agencies? Was their permission sought? If so what steps did they take to ensure that the whole demonstration was conducted peacefully? If their permission was not sought, what steps did they take to stop the demonstration from taking place? Or were they taken by surprise on Monday morning when they woke up and found some churches and Christian Social Centre filled with people?

Demonstrations certainly constitute one of the most dramatic ways of making a political statement. It brings one's cause to the fore, beyond the purview of those who would normally take a decision on the matter. Where one has a strong case and one suspects that justice may not be done, a demonstration puts the decision-makers on the spot. But the way demonstrations are organized and conducted makes a lot of difference in whether the much sought after sympathy would be gained or lost.

The Christian Association of Nigeria (CAN) leaders might have resorted to demonstration because they felt the State Assembly Committee's report was not going to favour them. And for that reason they concluded that *shari'a* was a fore-gone conclusion in Kaduna. They ignored the very important fact that the legislature, alone, does not constitute the government. There is the executive and the judiciary. If the CAN leadership had looked beyond the legislature it would have found in the state executive a listening ear. Did not Governor Ahmed Makarfi establish a bi-religious body co-chaired by a Christian and a Muslim cleric to advise him on the *sharia*? Is that indicative of somebody who had already made up his mind about what to do?

The capability of the law enforcement and security agencies in detecting and nipping in the bud unlawful activities is seriously called to question by their performance last week. Security agencies are supposed to be on the alert at all times and have their feelers everywhere. The security agencies could not have feigned ignorance of the impending demonstration of last Monday as circulars were sent to all churches in Kaduna, and Christians were invited in their tens of thousands to congregate at selected places at an appointed time.

The Kaduna State Police Commissioner is reported to have said that no permission was sought by the demonstrators before they embarked on the march. Granted that it was impossible at that time to seal off the premises they were occupying in order to prevent them from demonstrating. The next most reasonable thing to have been done was to get the organizers of the march to sign an undertaking to be held responsible for any breach of the peace that will result from their activities.

Indeed, the question of the propriety and even efficacy of a demonstration to make their point came up at the meeting of the Christian leadership. Some foresaw the peaceful demonstration getting out of control and cautioned against it.

There is ample evidence that the CAN leadership did deliberate on the possibility of the peaceful demonstration going out of control. But a faction of the Christian leadership, mostly CAN executives—the political wing of the church—thought that unless the message was sent loud and clear before the Assembly Committee wrote its report, it would be too late. The issue, as far as they were concerned, was whether to risk the imposition of *sharia* because they had not expressed their opposition strongly, even when there is the possibility of the process of that expression degenerating to violence. A few priests cautioned against the march. But they were over-ruled. Nonetheless, at their churches on Sunday, they advised their flock not to participate in the demonstration being called for the following day.

The spate of violent communal and religious crises in the country the last few decades is symptomatic of one problem: the failure of the state.

It is high time the state performed its reason for being. It is high time governments governed. It is high time the society gave to the state the support it requires to perform its roles. Governance is a contract. And in all contracts, it takes two to enter it and fulfill its obligations.

Unfortunately, in Nigeria, as in most Third World states, the contract is made to be one-sided. The state is expected at all times to meet its part of the contractual agreement—protect lives and property; enhance the living standard of the citizens, etc.—without a corresponding expectation on the part of the citizens, to render unto the state and indeed, other citizens their duties and responsibilities.

It is instructive to note that when some residents of some suburbs of Kaduna decided to fulfill their social responsibilities as citizens, they were able to ward off the rioters from their wards and quarters. At Kawo and Kabalan Doki, two suburbs of the city, Muslims and Christians forgot their religious differences and kept the rioters at bay. They did not wait for the police or soldiers to come, which would have been too late for them. If only we can all resolve to take our responsibilities to ourselves, our families, our community, our state, our nation and our God seriously, we shall save ourselves a lot of the trouble that we find ourselves in.

▲ NOTES

[1] Since these appendices are written by Nigerians, I remind you of my comments in the Introduction about the English used by some Nigerian writers. These appendices occasionally display this tendency. I have taken the liberty to standardize a few of the more obvious cases.

[2] A press statement by some lecturers of Ahmadu Bello University, Zaria, Friday, 13th March, 1987. This document has been appended to the CAN news release, "The 1987 Kaduna State Religious Disturbances: A Modern Day *Jihad* Being Inflicted on Nigeria," (1987?). A significant section of this document is interpretative and really belongs in one of the next volumes. However, since the group is an inter-religious one, it could not be classified under either Christian or Muslim. In addition, it is preferable to keep the document together. Hence it is appended to this

volume, but it will be referred to in some of the next volumes.

3 For information about this debate, see Boer, 1979, pp. 478ff and 1984, pp. 142ff.

4 This document is signed by 22 lecturers, both Christians and Muslims.

5 Only the relevant sections are reproduced. I have left most of the non-standard English intact.

6 This was the Gowon family house. Daniel's brother, Yakubu, is a former Head of State. Their parents lay buried in the front yard.

7 *NN*, 26 Feb/2000, pp. 4-5.

8 That is, a citizen of Niger, not of Nigeria.

9 *NN*, 27 Feb/2000, p. 13.

10 Acronym for "Government Residential Area," a colonial leftover somewhat equivalent to a suburb.

11 *NN*, 27 Feb/2000, p. 3.

BIBLIOGRAPHY

ABU Lecturers. "The Violent Politics of Religion and the Survival of Nigeria." Press Statement by a group of lecturers of Ahmadu Bello University, Zaria, 13 Mar/87. See Appendix 1.

Abdullahi, Bala and Kolade, Kayode. "Kaduna's Killing Fields." *NN*, 26 Feb/2000, pp. 4-5. Appendix 4.

Abdulsalami, Isa. "Armed Soldiers Deployed to Restore Peace to Jos." *Guardian*, 9 Sep/2001.

Achi, Lois and Peter-Omale, Funmi. "20 Feared Dead in Jos PDP Ward Congress Fracas." *TD*, 3 May/2002.

Alao, Onimisi. "Escalation of Rage." *NN*, 27 Feb/2000, p. 13. Appendix 5.

Anonymous. "Zangon Kataf Riots: The True Story." *TC* 3/92, pp. 4-11.

Asaju, Tunde and Oladipo, Dotun. "Mayhem." *Newswatch*, 6 Mar/2000, pp. 8-21.

Asaju, Tunde. "Counting Their Losses." *Newswatch*, 27 Mar/2000, pp. 28-30.

Audu, Solomon. "Ethno-Religious Disturbances in Jos." *Kutaya Forum*, Newsletter of the Messianic Support Group, Vol. 3, No. 2, pp. 1-2.

Awowede, Obed. "Cover Story." *Tell*, 6 Mar/2000, pp. 15-17, 19-20.

Babarinsa, Dare. "Allahu Akbar!" *Tell*, 28 Oct/91, pp. 12-16.

Boer, Jan H. *Missionary Messengers of Liberation in a Colonial Context: A Case Study of the Sudan United Mission*. Amsterdam Series of Theology, Vol. I. Amsterdam: Rodopi Editions, 1979.

————. *Missions: Heralds of Capitalism or Christ?* Ibadan: Daystar Press, 1984.

————. *Science Without Faith Is Dead*. Jos: Institute of Church & Society, 1991.

————. *Caught in the Middle: Christians in Transnational Corporations*. Jos: Institute of Church & Society, 1992.

————. Web site <www.SocialTheology.com>

Boer, Wiebe K. Private e-mail of 10 Sep/2001.

Bolt, John. *A Free Church, a Holy Nation: Abraham Kuyper's American Public Theology*. Grand Rapids: Eerdmans, 2001.

Bratt. James D. (Ed.). *Abraham Kuyper: A Centennial Reader*. Grand Rapids: Eerdmans, 1998.

Carpenter, Joel. "Neo-Calvinism and the Future of Religious Colleges." Insert in *Contact*, Newsletter of the International Association for the Promotion of Christian Higher Education, March 2001, p. 2. This article is soon to appear in *The Future of Religious Colleges* by Eerdmans.

Christian Association of Nigeria, Kano State Branch. *30th October, 1982. Kano Religious Disturbance Memorandum.* Kano: CAN, 1982.

———. *Leadership in Nigeria: An Analysis.* Enlightenment Series 1. Kaduna: CAN Publicity Committee, Northern Zone, 1987 (?).

———. Ten Northern States. Release: "The 1987 Kaduna State Religious Disturbances: A Modern Day Jihad Being Inflicted on Nigeria." 1987.

———. Jema'a Local Government Branch. "Situation Report on Religious Disturbance in Kafanchan as at 12:00 Midnight of 11th March, 1987." Appendix B, CAN Release, 1987.

Dandaura, J. H. Letter to the Secretary of the Committee Appointed to Investigate the Religious Disturbance of 30th October, 1982. 3 Dec/82.

Debki, B.E.E. *The Tragedy of Sharia: Kaduna Crisis from an Eyewitness.* Kaduna: Self-published, 2000.

Dirambi, Audu. "Government Must Wake up to Her Responsibilities," an interview. *TC,* 3/95, pp. 25-26.

Director, Osa. "Nigeria's Hidden War: Bloodbath in Bauchi State." *TELL,* 8 Jan/96, pp. 6-9.

Falola, Toyin. *Violence in Nigeria: The Crisis of Religious Politics* and *Secular Ideologies.* Rochester: University of Rochester Press, 1998.

Garba, L. "Report on the Clash between Muslim and Christian Students of the College of Education, Kafanchan, on 6 March, 1987." Attached to CAN Release of 1987 as Appendix A.

Gedege, (initials not known). "Kano Needs Divine Intervention," an interview. *TC,* 3/95, pp. 23-24.

Gibb, H. A. R. *Modern Trends in Islam*. New York: Octagon, 1975.

Glynn, Patrick. *God the Evidence: The Reconciliation of Faith and Reason in a Postsecular World*. Grand Rapids: Eerdmans, 1995.

Gowon, Daniel D. "Submission to the Kaduna State Commission of Enquiry into the Recent Disturbances in Kaduna State." N.d. See Appendix 2.

The Grand Design. The Quarterly Journal of the Nigeria Christian Graduate Fellowship (Zaria Branch). Vol. I, No. 3: (n.d.).

Grissen, Lillian V. *That We May Be One: The Autobiography of Nigerian Ambassador Jolly Tanko Yusuf*. Grand Rapids: Eerdmans, 1995.

Gwadah, Yusuf. "Death and Destruction at Baptist Seminary, Kaduna, in 2000." Privately circulated report. Appendix 3.

Heslam, Peter S. *Creating a Christian Worldview: Abraham Kuyper's Lectures on Calvinism*. Grand Rapids: Eerdmans, 1998.

Igiebor, Nosa. "From the Editor." *Tell*, 6 Mar/2000, p. 13.

Jega, M. "Zangon-Kataf Riot: The Road to Hell." *Citizen,* 15-21 June, 1992, pp. 11-16.

Kantiok, James B. *Muslims and Christians in Northern Nigeria: Political and Cultural Implications for Evangelism*. Unpublished dissertation manuscript for Fuller Theological Seminary, 1999.

Kukah, Matthew H. *Religion, Politics and Power in Northern Nigeria*. Ibadan: Spectrum Books, 1993.

Kumm, H.K.W. *The Sudan: A Short Compendium of Facts and Figures about the Land of Darkness*. London: Marshall Brothers, 1907.

Kuyper, Abraham. *Het sociale vraagstuk en de Christelijke religie*. See James W. Skillen's edited translation, *The Problem of Poverty*.

Grand Rapids: Baker Book House, 1991.

―――. *Lectures in Calvinism.* Grand Rapids: Eerdmans, 1931. (Stone Lectures at Princeton University, 1889).

Lugo, Luis E. (Ed.) *Religion, Pluralism, and Public Life: Abraham Kuyper's Legacy for the Twenty-First Century.* Grand Rapids: Eerdmans, 1998.

Madaki, Yohanna A. "For the Records: On the Plight of the Sayawa: From Madaki to Raji." *TC,* No. 1/96, pp. 9–13.

―――. "Christians Can Only Fight the Devil if…." *TC,* No. 1/97, pp. 10–13.

Maier, Karl. *This House Has Fallen: Midnight in Nigeria.* New York: Public Affairs, 2000.

Marshall, Paul. *Their Blood Cries Out: The Worldwide Tragedy of Modern Christians Who Are Dying for Their Faith.* Dallas: Word Publishing, 1997.

McGoldrick, James E. *Abraham Kuyper: God's Renaissance Man.* Darlington, UK: Evangelical Press, 2000.

Minchakpu, Obed B. "Ghosts Haunt Kano." *TC.* No. 3/95, pp. 16-18.

―――. "Sayawa Christians on Trial." *TC,* No. 1/96, pp. 6-8.

―――. "Manal-Widowed at 23: A Victim of Violence in Nigeria" and other stories. *CC,* 7 Aug/2000, p. 5.

―――. "200 Christians Killed in Nigeria's Bauchi State." *CC,* 29 Oct/2001.

―――. "Five Hundred Killed in Religious Conflict in Nigeria." *CC,* 26 Aug/2002, p. 8.

Ndiomu, Charles (Director). *Religious Disturbances in Nigeria.* Kuru: The National Institute for Policy and Strategic Studies, 1986.

New Nigerian (Kaduna). Miscellaneous editions.

Nigeria Standard (Jos). Miscellaneous editions.

Obasanjo, Olusegan. Broadcast to the nation, 12 Mar/2000. *Newswatch*, 13 Mar/2000, pp. 22-26.

Obassa, Shittu. "Horrors of Kaduna." *NN*, 26 Feb/2000, p. 7.

Ojudu, Babafemi. Interview with Yakubu Yahaya: "I Am Not Afraid of Death." *African Concord*, 22 Apr/1991, pp. 36-37.

Oladipo, Dotun. "Obasanjo's Tough Stance on Sharia." *Newswatch*, 13 Mar/2000, pp. 20-28.

Olesanmi, Simeon O. *Religious Pluralism and the Nigerian State.* Monographs in International Studies. Africa Series, No. 66. Athens: Ohio University Center for International Studies, 1997.

Olupona, Jacob K., ed. *Religion and Peace in Multi-Faith Nigeria.* Published by the editor, 1992.

Omotunde, D. "Tyranny of the Fanatical." Editorial. *Tell* 28 Oct/91, p. 3.

Onaiyekan, J. "Religious Tolerance and Peaceful Coexistence among Nigerians." *Encounter* (Rome), Apr/85, pp. 1-12.

Rabo, Emmanuel S. "Remembering Sharia Widows." *TC*, 1/2001, pp. 26-27.

Sanda, Umar. "Avoidable Carnage in Kaduna." *NN*, 27 Feb/2000, p. 3. Appendix 6.

Stevens, R. Paul. "The Marketplace: Mission Field or Mission?" *Crux: Quarterly Journal of Christian Thought and Opinion.*

Vancouver: Regent College, Sep/2001, pp. 7-16.

The Sunday Magazine (TSM), 27 Sep/92, 14 Feb/93.

Sunday Tribune, 16 Apr/89.

TEKAN. *Towards the Right Path for Nigeria*. Jos: TEKAN, 1987.

Tell. Miscellaneous issues.

Tidings, No. 2, 1987.

Today's Challenge (Jos). Miscellaneous issues.

Tsado, Jacob and Ari, Yusufu. "Special Investigation: Who Is Trying to Destabilise Islam?" *TC*, 4/87, pp. 16-20, 32.

Uche, Samuel. "Is Islam Lawlessness?" An interview. *TC*, 3/96, pp. 20-22.

Van Der Walt, Bennie. *The Liberating Message: A Christian Worldview for Africa*. Postchefstroom: Potschefstroom University for Christian Higher Education, 1994.

Wase, Muhammed. "We Have No Place for Mischievous Elements in Kano." *TC*, 3/95, p. 19.

Wilson-Smith, Anthony. "Faith for Ever after—or No More." *Maclean's*, 17 Dec/2001, p. 2.

Wolterstorff, Nicholas. *Reason within the Bounds of Religion*. Grand Rapids: Eerdmans, 1976.

Wootton, R. W. E., ed. *Jesus—More Than a Prophet*. Leicester: Intervarsity, 1982.

Wudiri, Ayuba J. "An Appeal to the Federal Military Government of Nigeria: Call *The New Nigerian* Newspapers and Agents of Destabilization to Order Now." A stenciled open letter. 24 Oct/88.

Yusuf, J.T. *That We May Be One: The Autobiography of Nigerian Ambassador Jolly Tanko Yusuf.* As told to Lillian V. Grissen. Grand Rapids: Eerdmans, 1995.

INDEX